Word Search
PUZZLES
for
Young
Einsteins

by Helene Hovanec

Sterling Publishing Co., Inc.
New York, N.Y

Edited by Claire Bazinet

3 5 7 9 10 8 6 4
Published by Sterling Publishing Co., Inc.
387 Park Avenue South, New York, N.Y. 10016
© 2001 by Helene Hovanec
Distributed in Canada by Sterling Publishing
c/o Canadian Manda Group, 165 Dufferin Street,
Toronto, Ontario, Canada M6K 3H6
Distributed in Great Britain and Europe by Chris Lloyd at Orca Book
Services, Stanley House, Fleets Lane, Poole BH15 3AJ, England
Distributed in Australia by Capricorn Link (Australia) Pty. Ltd.
P.O. Box 704, Windsor, NSW 2756 Australia
Printed in Hong Kong

Sterling ISBN 0-8069-5849-9

Contents

Welcome

Sometimes I go to schools and present puzzle programs to groups of children. Whenever I ask my audience to tell me their favorite puzzle types, they usually say "word searches" because "they're easy."

I agree. Regular word searches are quite simple to do. You're given a list of words and all you have to do is hunt through the diagram and circle each one after you find it. Piece of cake!

Well, in *Word Search Puzzles for Young Einsteins* things are a little different. Sure, you still get to search through the letters to find words but, in each of these puzzles, you get more. Something to do either before or after your word search, to make things more interesting.

For example, in "Hidden Riddles" you get to read the leftover letters to find the answer to a riddle. (Feel free to groan or giggle after you do that!)

In "Missing Letters" you need to figure out which letter was removed from each listed word before finding that new word in the grid. In "Found Letters" you must decide which letter was added to the listed word, and search for the larger word in the grid.

With each puzzle, you'll be given a special set of instructions. But the basics of word searching the grids are the same: look across, up, down, and diagonally, both forward and backward. Circle each word (or phrase) when you find it.

Happy solving!

Helene Hovanec

Solving Hints

Here are a few hints to help you solve these word search puzzles.

For puzzles where there's a hidden answer:
- *Be sure* to circle every word listed, no matter how small it is.
- *Don't* circle any words that are not in the list.
- Circle each word *carefully* so you'll be able to see the leftover letters and read the riddle answer.

For puzzles like "Synonym Search," "Opposite Distraction," etc., where you have to find words that are not listed, here's a hint: It's true that the puzzle's word list is not in alphabetical order, but the answer words are. So, when you can't come up with an answer, looking at the answer just above and below the one you need will provide you with a good clue.

For all puzzles: If you think you're stumped on a puzzle, don't just stop and give up. Use reference books, ask your parents or friends for help, even take a quick peek at the answers to get you going again. It's okay. A puzzle is, after all, only a game. And, if you take time to figure out the answers this time around, even with help, guess what? Next time, you may know the answers!

Insect Aside

After you find 16 insects, read the *leftover* letters from left to right and top to bottom to answer this riddle: Why was the insect kicked out of the national park? Write the answers in the spaces at the bottom.

APHID
BEETLE
BOLL WEEVIL
CICADA
FIREFLY
FLEA
GNAT
HORNET
KATYDID
LOCUST
MIDGE
MOSQUITO
MOTH
ROACH
TERMITE
TICK

B	O	L	L	W	E	E	V	I	L
H	T	O	M	B	E	L	C	A	Y
U	I	D	I	D	Y	T	A	K	L
S	U	H	O	R	N	E	T	E	F
L	Q	C	C	I	T	E	I	T	E
O	S	A	W	I	A	B	C	S	R
C	O	O	M	A	C	L	K	I	I
U	M	R	T	T	E	A	E	L	F
S	E	R	B	U	E	G	D	I	M
T	A	N	G	D	I	H	P	A	G

Answer: __ _ _ _ _ _ _ _   _ _   _ _ _ _ _ _   _

_ _ _ _ _ _ _ _ _ _

Answer on page 84.

Follow the Leader #1

Find a string of connected words in the grid. Start with **GOOD** (which is circled for you) and then find a 4-letter word that starts with the **D** in **GOOD**. After you find the second word, look for the third word. It starts with **H** and has four letters. The list below will guide you. Continue in this way until you've found the last word, which will be related to **GOOD**.

1. GOOD
2. D _ _ _
3. H _ _ _
4. P _ _ _ _ _ _
5. Y _ _ _ _
6. K _ _ _ _ _ _ _ _
7. G _ _
8. M _ _ _ _ _ _
9. W _ _ _ _ _ _
10. R _ _ _
11. K _ _ _ _
12. B _ _ _ _ _
13. D _ _ _
14. P _ _ _
15. N _ _ _ _ _
16. R _ _ _ _ _
17. S _ _ _ _ _ _
18. G _ _ _ _
19. M _ _ _ _ _
20. L _ _ _ _

```
S Y M L G Y H Y M G
T Y G E K E S H O V
G W T C L G A O M W
N C U P H L D P Z L
I L R R V R O Z A G
S Z A E Y R Z W R N
S P H T D L A O E O
I J B T E N O V Q R
K N A Y D M E X A T
L S H E G R O L E S
P V R I S K N O B Y
```

Answer on page 90.

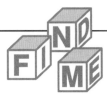

Central Station

Each two-letter word in the box below will fit into the blank spaces on each line to form the *end* of one word and the *start* of another word. Place each small word into its correct spot and then find all 38 new words in the grid on the opposite page. Cross off each word as you use it. We did one set for you.

~~AD~~	AL	BE	EL
EX	GO	HE	ID
IN	IT	LA	LO
MA	ME	NO	OF
	ON	OR	SO

1. A C T _ _   _ _ D E R
2. A N N _ _   _ _ A C T
3. B A T _ _   _ _ A R T
4. C A B _ _   _ _ N E R
5. C A M _ _   _ _ B O W
6. C E L _ _   _ _ B B Y
7. C H I _ _   _ _ S S Y
8. C O M _ _   _ _ J O R
9. C O R _ _   _ _ L O W
10. F A T _ _   _ _ R R Y

11. F R U _ _   _ _ C H Y
12. G L O _ _   _ _ A R D
13. P I A _ _   _ _ R T H
14. P L A _ _   _ _ I O T
15. P R O _ _   _ _ T E N
16. S A L A <u>D</u>   <u>A</u> <u>D</u> O P T
17. T A N _ _   _ _ O S E
18. V I L _ _   _ _ T E R
19. W A G _ _   _ _ I O N

Answer on page 87.

```
F  G  L  O  S  T  A  F  O  O  R  P  L  N
L  H  A  B  R  Q  B  A  T  H  E  X  O  O
Y  M  R  J  E  M  I  H  C  T  T  G  B  I
R  H  O  X  D  A  T  F  P  L  A  A  B  N
R  Y  C  Q  R  W  R  P  L  W  L  N  Y  O
O  W  E  T  O  U  A (D  A  L  A  S) G  Z
S  O  L  Z  I  N  E  Z  I  N  N  E  R  O
T  B  L  T  S  X  H  V  D  D  P  P  N  F
G  L  O  B  E  V (T) R  B  H  I  R  G  T
M  E  X  N  Q  S (P) C  L  A  L  O  H  E
L  R  N  A  C  T (O) R  N  E  S  Y  T  N
C  A  M  G  V  M (D) O  M  A  J  O  R  T
Y  S  S  E  M  Z (A) A  G  A  L  L  O  W
N  I  B  A  C  T  C  A  X  E  X  T  N  R
```

9

Synonym Search #1

Don't look for these listed words in the grid. Instead, look for a synonym of each word. For example, **ACTOR**, a synonym for **PERFORMER**, is in the grid, and we've circled it for you. Write the new words on the blank lines.

1. PERFORMER _____ACTOR_____
2. GROWN-UP _____
3. REPLY _____
4. INFANT _____
5. ANIMAL _____
6. BUZZER _____
7. TASK _____
8. PAIR _____
9. PROM _____
10. PEP _____
11. MISTAKE _____
12. HAPPENING _____
13. GUY _____
14. MOVIE _____
15. PASTIME _____
16. LAMP _____
17. HARPOON _____
18. TEAM _____
19. TALE _____
20. AVENUE _____
21. WORKPLACE _____
22. CAB _____
23. INSTRUCTOR _____

Answer on page 88.

```
B  A  B  Y  T  N  E  V  E  E  E
B  E  Z  A  N  S  W  E  R  V
Q  E  A  J  H  T  R  R  O  T
T  N  L  S  L  O  O  V  H  E
A  E  T  L  T  R  B  G  C  A
X  R  E  C  Z  Y  I  B  W  C
I  G  A  R  O  L  Q  X  Y  H
Y  Y  D  S  T  U  D  I  O  E
S  Q  U  A  D  S  P  E  A  R
F  I  L  M  F  E  L  L  O  W
Q  G  T  P  D  A  N  C  E  L
```

Hear Ye! #1

A homophone is a word that sounds just like another word, but is spelled differently and has a different meaning. Look at each word in the list and find its homophone in the grid. For example, **CHORD** is listed, but **CORD** is in the grid. Write the new words on the blank lines.

1. CHORD _____CORD_____
2. FARE _____
3. FOR _____
4. HERE _____
5. HEAL _____
6. HORSE _____
7. OUR _____
8. MALE _____
9. MAIN _____
10. MISSED _____
11. KNEW _____
12. PLAIN _____
13. PORE _____

14. RAYS _____
15. RAIN _____
16. CHUTE _____
17. SLEIGH _____
18. SUM _____
19. SOLE _____
20. THERE _____
21. TOE _____
22. HOLY _____
23. ONE _____
24. WOOD _____
25. RAP _____
26. RIGHT _____

Answer on page 84.

```
S  N  Q  H  E  E  L  E  S  H
O  N  G  I  E  R  N  N  O  W
M  A  I  L  H  A  M  A  U  R
E  Q  A  O  T  L  R  M  L  A
F  H  U  R  H  S  W  B  T  P
W  R  I  T  E  G  H  W  R  O
D  A  S  C  I  R  O  O  T  U
F  I  Z  O  R  U  L  X  O  R
M  S  H  R  L  O  L  Z  W  T
N  E  W  D  J  F  Y  A  L  S
```

Missing Letters #1

One letter was removed from each word in the list before it was put into the grid. Example: **SHAME** is in the list, the **H** was removed, and **SAME** was circled. Find all the new words, circle them, and write the missing letter on the line. When you've found all the words, read the missing letters from 1 to 19 to answer this riddle: Why did the monster nibble on the electric bulb? Write the answer in the spaces under the grid.

1. SHAME __H__
2. BEACON _____
3. SWERVE _____
4. LAUNCH _____
5. MENTAL _____
6. JOINTS _____
7. FEATHER _____
8. POWDER _____
9. CHAIN _____
10. BLEACH _____
11. COPIES _____
12. BRIDGE _____
13. THREAT _____
14. HEARTS _____
15. BOAST _____
16. PRINCE _____
17. TAINT _____
18. SCARCE _____
19. MONKEY _____

F	B	E	A	C	H	C	N	U	L
Z	A	M	B	H	E	A	R	S	A
L	C	T	X	I	L	T	I	N	T
W	O	Z	H	N	B	J	J	Z	E
T	N	Y	Q	E	W	O	M	N	M
A	P	M	S	B	R	I	D	E	O
E	C	O	P	E	S	N	S	R	N
R	G	Z	W	T	R	S	A	A	E
T	A	O	B	X	Y	V	M	C	Y
V	P	R	I	C	E	M	E	S	R

Answer: __ __ __ __ __ __ __ __ __

     __ __ __ __ __ __ __ __ __ __

Answer on page 91.

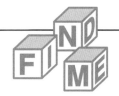

Do-Re-Mi

Find 27 terms related to money in the diagram. Then read the *leftover* letters from left to right and top to bottom to finish this riddle: Why is the stack of money crying to the bank manager? Because . . . Write the answer in the spaces below.

ASSET
BOND
CAPITAL
CASH
CENT
CHECK
COIN
COUPON
DIME
DIVIDEND
DOLLAR
DOUGH
EQUITY
FUND
GELT
GOLD
MOOLAH
NICKEL
PENNY
PORTFOLIO
QUARTER
QUOTE
RATE
SHARE
SILVER
STOCK
TRUST

S	D	T	C	A	S	H	G	U	O	D
H	I	I	E	T	A	R	H	D	O	I
A	M	L	T	S	T	W	A	L	P	V
R	E	A	V	S	S	N	L	O	O	I
E	L	T	U	E	S	A	O	G	R	D
T	A	R	K	P	R	O	O	B	T	E
N	T	E	C	A	E	S	M	L	F	N
I	I	C	E	N	T	N	E	U	O	D
C	P	O	H	O	R	G	N	L	L	N
K	A	O	C	A	A	D	N	Y	I	O
E	C	K	C	O	U	P	O	N	O	B
L	Y	T	I	U	Q	E	T	O	U	Q

Answer: __ __   __ __ __ __ __ __   __ __

__ __ __   __ __ __ __

Answer on page 92.

Anagrams #1

Each word in the list can be anagrammed—its letters rearranged to form a new word. First, figure out the new word. (Use the starting letter we've provided as a hint.) Then, find each new word in the grid on the opposite page and circle it. Remember, in an anagram *all letters* of the original word will be used. The first one is done for you.

1.	STAB	BATS	**13.**	LISTEN	S	
2.	CALM	C	**14.**	STREAK	S	
3.	SOURCE	C	**15.**	OURS	S	
4.	GREAT	G	**16.**	SATIN	S	
5.	EARTH	H	**17.**	STALE	S	
6.	REGAL	L	**18.**	DRIEST	S	
7.	DEALER	L	**19.**	TEXAS	T	
8.	VOLLEY	L	**20.**	SHEET	T	
9.	NERVE	N	**21.**	HORNET	T	
10.	STEP	P	**22.**	WORTH	T	
11.	MARINE	R	**23.**	CATER	T	
12.	HOSE	S				

Answer on page 86.

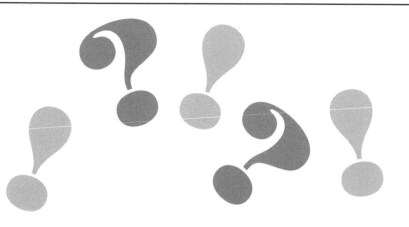

```
H  E  A  R  T  R  A  C  E  L
N  N  E  V  E  R  C  W  X  L
I  I  W  T  N  L  O  B  L  O
A  G  A  V  A  R  U  A  E  V
T  K  M  M  H  H  R  T  A  E
S  H  L  T  E  G  S  S  D  L
P  Q  R  A  E  R  E  I  E  Y
E  S  H  O  E  A  R  Z  R  J
S  I  L  E  N  T  A  X  E  S
T  T  H  E  S  E  S  O  U  R
```

Choices #1

Three words on each line look similar. Choose the one that matches the definition given and find only *that* word in the grid on the opposite page. Work back and forth between the grid and the word list if you're not sure of some definitions.

1. AERIAL - AEROSPACE - AEROSOL — TV antenna
2. COMMENCE - COMMENT - COMMIT — Begin
3. GARNISH - GARNET - GARMENT — Piece of clothing
4. HAMMER - HALVE - HAMPER — Get in the way of
5. HARDEN - HARASS - HARMONIZE — Annoy someone again and again
6. NAUGHTY - NATURAL - NAUTICAL — Not artificial
7. PICNIC - PLANKTON - PANIC — Fear
8. PARASOL - PARCEL - PARASITE — Small umbrella
9. PIONEER - PINTO - PINAFORE — Girl's dress
10. PITCHFORK - PITCHER - PITFALL — Container for liquids
11. POLKA - POLO - POLLEN — Folk dance
12. PROBE - PROCEED - PROFIT — Investigate carefully
13. PUBLIC - PUNGENT - PUNCTUAL — On time
14. QUITE - QUAINT - QUIET — Old-fashioned
15. RECESS - RECIPE - RECEIPT — Proof of purchase
16. RIPPLE - RIVAL - RITUAL — Competitor
17. RADISH - RUBBER - RUBBISH — Trash
18. SQUIRE - SQUIRT - SQUIRM — Wriggle
19. STATUTE - STATURE - STATUE — A law
20. SUNDAY - SUNSPOT - SUNDAE — Ice cream treat
21. TERRITORY - TERRACE - TERMITE — Small insect
22. TRAITOR - TRAINER - TRAILER — Instructor

Answer on page 88.

23.	TROUPE - TRUCE - TRUANT	Student who skips school
24.	TURNPIKE - TURNSTILE - TURNTABLE	Toll road for cars
25.	VAIN - VACANT - VALIANT	Not occupied
26.	VANISH - VARNISH - VANQUISH	Disappear
27.	WITHDRAWN - WISTFUL - WITTY	Not friendly
28.	WRITHE - WRINKLE - WRING	Crease
29.	ZINNIA - ZIPPER - ZITHER	Garden flower

```
W  P  A  N  I  C  O  M  M  E  N  C  E  Q  E
M  U  J  X  Y  V  D  N  E  T  E  R  P  G  L
T  N  A  U  R  T  A  K  R  Z  P  R  T  A  K
P  C  N  V  S  T  I  N  I  P  O  E  I  R  N
I  T  C  H  U  P  G  N  I  B  G  R  M  M  I
E  U  M  R  N  W  N  T  E  S  E  O  V  E  R
C  A  A  R  D  I  C  S  E  A  H  F  A  N  W
E  L  U  S  A  H  R  Q  T  R  A  A  C  T  I
R  T  J  R  E  Q  L  U  N  D  M  N  A  K  T
B  E  O  R  U  B  B  I  S  H  P  I  N  L  H
Z  M  N  A  I  E  N  R  R  A  E  P  T  Y  D
A  Q  I  I  R  V  Z  M  X  R  R  N  Y  E  R
F  N  J  T  A  M  A  T  Z  A  K  L  O  P  A
T  Y  H  D  L  R  N  L  O  S  A  R  A  P  W
R  V  S  E  T  U  T  A  T  S  T  H  S  Y  N
```

First Names (She)

The last names of some famous women (both past and present) are listed below. Next to each name there's a short description of each one's claim to fame. Write each first name in the blank space and then find that name in the grid on the opposite page.

1. _____ Earhart (first woman to fly a plane across the Atlantic Ocean)

2. _____ Frank (Jewish girl with a famous diary)

3. _____ Ross (sewed the first American flag)

4. _____ Clinton (daughter of the 42nd president of the U.S.)

5. _____ Barton (Civil War nurse; organized American Red Cross)

6. _____ Ross (singer with the Supremes)

7. _____ Barrymore (actress who starred in "E.T." when she was eight years old)

8. _____ Dickinson (American poet)

9. _____ O'Keeffe (noted for her paintings of flowers; her first name is the same as a southern state)

10. _____ Keller (born blind and deaf, she learned to read, write, and use sign language)

11. _____ Jackson (singer whose brother is Michael)

12. _____ Curie (physicist who discovered radium)

13. _____ Washington (wife of the first president)

14. _____ Shelley (author of *Frankenstein*)

15. _____ Hamm (soccer player)

16. _____ Pitcher (supplied water Revolutionary War soldiers)

17. _____ Winfrey (has a very popular talk show)

Answer on page 86.

18. _____ Carson (wrote about dangers of pollution in *Silent Spring*)

19. _____ Parks (Afro-American woman who refused to give up her bus seat to a white man)

20. _____ Ride (first American women to go into space)

21. _____ Lipinski (ice skater who won a gold medal at 1994 Olympics)

22. _____ Williams (tennis player whose name sounds like a planet)

A	E	S	L	E	H	C	Y	H	M
Z	N	E	L	E	H	A	R	P	O
Q	R	N	A	I	G	R	O	E	G
S	U	N	E	V	A	M	I	A	M
A	V	Y	M	M	A	R	T	H	A
L	W	S	I	I	A	A	A	L	R
L	W	T	L	M	S	C	R	L	Y
Y	V	E	Y	O	X	H	A	J	C
X	M	B	R	J	T	E	N	A	J
A	N	A	I	D	Y	L	L	O	M

Opposite Distraction

None of these listed words will be found in the grid. Instead, look for the word that means the *opposite* of the one on the list. For example, **ANTIQUE** is circled, because it's the opposite of **MODERN**. Write the new words on each line and then circle each one on the grid.

1. MODERN   ANTIQUE

2. FILTHY _____

3. VAGUE _____

4. EXCELLENT _____

5. LIGHT _____

6. FULL _____

7. TRUE _____

8. CORRUPT _____

9. CRUEL _____

10. FIRST _____

11. DIFFERENT _____

12. NEAT _____

13. MAJOR _____

14. LEAST _____

15. MEAN _____

16. RUDE _____

17. ABSENT _____

18. SLOW _____

19. FREQUENT _____

20. HARD _____

21. LASTING _____

Answer on page 84.

```
J  K  R  A  D  N  I  K  C  E
G  H  F  W  X  I  P  C  K  G
R  R  A  T  Y  C  O  I  C  P
O  A  L  S  R  E  L  U  R  R
N  R  S (A  N  T  I  Q  U  E)
I  E  E  M  S  A  T  B  M  S
M  L  S  M  D  T  E  P  M  E
C  H  O  N  E  S  T  L  Y  N
L  S  O  F  T  Y  G  M  C  T
T  E  M  P  O  R  A  R  Y  P
```

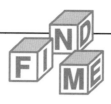

House Hunting

After you find 20 places to live, read the *leftover* letters from left to right and top to bottom to answer this riddle: Why didn't the witch buy the house she really liked? Write the answers in the spaces at the bottom.

APARTMENT
BUNGALOW
CABIN
CASTLE
CAVE
COTTAGE
DORM
DUPLEX
FARM
HOTEL
IGLOO
LODGE
MANOR
MANSION
MOTEL
SHACK
TENT
TRAILER
VILLA
WIGWAM

R	T	M	T	H	E	R	M	R	A	F
E	C	R	E	K	C	A	H	S	E	W
L	D	O	N	H	N	A	S	E	M	W
I	U	D	T	O	N	I	G	L	O	O
A	P	A	R	T	M	E	N	T	T	L
R	L	C	O	E	A	B	V	S	E	A
T	E	A	R	L	O	G	O	A	L	G
M	X	B	L	O	D	G	E	C	C	N
C	W	I	G	W	A	M	L	O	S	U
E	V	N	O	I	S	N	A	M	T	B

Answer: _ _ _ _ _ _ _ _ _ _ _ _ _ _ _ _

_ _ _ _ _ _ _

Answer on page 89.

Found Letters #1

One letter was added to each word in the list before it was put into the grid. Example: **COUNTY** is in the list, the **R** was added, and **COUNTRY** was circled. Find all the new words, circle them, and write the added letter on the line. When you've found all the words, read the found letters from 1 to 19 to finish this riddle: Why did Lassie's owner use Wisk? To get rid of . . . Write the answer on the blanks at the bottom.

1. COUNTY __R__
2. MOVE _____
3. BAKERS _____
4. RUNS _____
5. PINT _____
6. BUNCH _____
7. CARTON _____
8. POND _____
9. MOTHS _____
10. INNER _____
11. HOSED _____
12. CAT _____
13. CARTS _____
14. ENTER _____
15. SHUT _____
16. CAMP _____
17. PACES _____
18. PLOT _____
19. SNAKY _____

```
C  A  R  T  O  O  N  R  P  P
H  O  S  T  E  D  E  A  M  I
P  O  U  N  D  T  I  M  A  L
L  X  Y  N  N  N  O  O  L  O
A  T  H  E  T  V  L  N  C  T
C  D  C  V  I  R  M  T  A  U
E  S  N  E  A  K  Y  H  R  O
S  R  U  N  G  S  C  S  E  H
B  Y  R  E  N  N  I  D  T  S
C  Q  B  A  N  K  E  R  S  J
```

Answer: __ __ __ __ __ __ __ __ __

__ __ __ __ __ __ __ __ __

Answer on page 86.

Best Quest #1

Check out your rhyming skills here. For each word in the list, there is a word that rhymes with it hidden in the grid. For example, **WAIT** is listed, but **BAIT** is in the grid. In this puzzle, each hidden word has the same ending as the word in the list. (There's a harder rhyme find on page 80.) Write the new words on the blank lines

1. WAIT ___BAIT___

2. FARMS _____

3. RIDER _____

4. MATTER _____

5. WAVY _____

6. LAVA _____

7. FUDGE _____

8. SMUGGLER _____

9. CRAZY _____

10. LATCH _____

11. RAVE _____

12. GRACE _____

13. MEAT _____

14. QUAKE _____

15. QUIVERING _____

16. READY _____

17. WITCHES _____

18. PREACHER _____

19. GRAVEL _____

20. PLUCK _____

21. ALLEY _____

22. HERB _____

Answer on page 95.

G Z P B G M T R U C K

R U F R M R P A V E J

G E A E A F A T T E R

N C T V Z W T V X G E

I A E Q A E C T Y D L

R L A Z K Y H R Y U G

E P C A D X E V Z J G

V R H A L D J L A S U

I S E (T I A B) M L E J

H T R C H A R M S A Z

S T I T C H E S Y T V

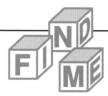

Flower Power

After you find 22 types of flower, read the *leftover* letters from left to right and top to bottom to answer this riddle: What's the definition of a black-eyed Susan? Write the answer in the spaces at the bottom.

BUTTERCUP
DAHLIA
FLAX
GARDENIA
GERANIUM
IRIS
JONQUIL
LAVENDER
LILAC
LILY
LOTUS
LUPINE
MUM
ORCHID
PANSY
PEONY
PETUNIA
POPPY
ROSE
TULIP
VIOLA
VIOLET

D	A	F	Y	C	P	D	T	A	I	S	L
A	D	L	N	Y	A	M	U	M	T	E	A
H	I	A	O	H	N	L	L	A	N	A	V
L	H	X	E	Y	S	A	I	I	J	I	E
I	C	T	P	L	Y	N	P	L	O	N	N
A	R	P	O	H	E	U	A	L	N	U	D
S	O	T	B	D	L	E	E	E	Q	T	E
P	U	C	R	E	T	T	U	B	U	E	R
S	N	A	I	N	S	I	R	I	I	P	A
F	G	I	S	A	L	O	I	V	L	T	F
I	G	M	U	I	N	A	R	E	G	H	T

Answer: __ _ _ _ _ _ _ _ _ _ _ _

_ _ _ _ _ _ _ _ _ _

Answer on page 88.

28

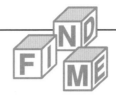

Birds of a Feather

After you've found this list of 19 birds in the grid, read the *leftover* letters from left to right and top to bottom to answer this riddle: What did one tropical bird say to the other tropical bird? Write the answer in the spaces below.

CANARY
CONDOR
COOT
CROW
CUCKOO
DODO
DOVE
EAGLE
FALCON
FINCH
GULL
LARK
LOON
MALLARD
ORIOLE
OWL
PIGEON
ROBIN
WOODPECKER

T	N	O	C	L	A	F	T	O	W
O	U	W	E	L	O	I	R	O	O
O	D	L	C	A	G	N	R	N	O
C	O	O	K	C	U	C	P	C	D
O	L	A	V	Y	L	H	A	A	P
N	L	T	T	E	L	N	H	I	E
D	R	A	L	L	A	M	G	L	C
O	O	G	R	R	A	E	O	T	K
R	A	D	Y	K	O	O	G	A	E
E	M	E	O	N	N	I	B	O	R

Answer: "_ _ _ _ _ _ _ _ _ _

_ _ _ _ _ _ _ _ _ _"

Answer on page 84.

Time Out

Fill in the blank space on each line with a word about holidays—those days when you celebrate something or honor someone. Then find each word in the grid on the opposite page. Take some time out to celebrate after you're done!

1. It's okay to kid around on _____ Fool's Day.

2. Plant trees on _____ Day.

3. The month of _____ has no major holidays.

4. A _____, or holiday song, is also a girl's name.

5. On October 12th, we honor _____, the explorer who discovered America.

6. Will _____ shoot an arrow into your heart on February 12th?

7. _____ and Dancer are on Santa's team.

8. Adults cast their ballots on _____ Day.

9. Honor your _____ on his special day in June.

10. The sky is lit up with _____ on the Fourth of July.

11. Wear red, white, and blue to celebrate _____ Day on June 14th.

12. The Jewish Festival of Lights is also known as _____.

13. July 4th is called _____ Day.

14. Afro-Americans celebrate _____ in late December.

15. Workers are honored on _____, which falls in September. (2 words)

16. The 16th president, Abraham _____, is one of the honorees on Presidents' Day.

17. January 15th is the day to honor Martin _____ King, the civil rights leader.

18. _____ 17th is the day to celebrate #24.

19. _____ honors those soldiers who died for their country. (2 words)

20. This candle holder, or _____, is used during the holiday in #12.

21. Honor thy _____ on her special day in May.

Answer on page 90.

22. There are many _____ on New Year's Day, but the most famous one is associated with the Rose Bowl in Pasadena.

23. _____ used his red nose to guide Santa on his journey.

24. People wear green on _____ Patrick's Day.

25. Dr. _____ invented the grinch who stole Christmas.

26. People who dream of a white Christmas are hoping that it will _____ .

27. Kids hang up their _____ on Christmas Eve and hope Santa will stuff them.

28. Collect oodles of candy by saying _____ on October 31. (3 words)

29. Millions of people eat _____ on Thanksgiving Day. (Gobble, gobble!)

30. The service people who fought in wars are remembered on _____ Day.

```
Y F I R E W O R K S E U S S
A S G N I K C O T S B C W E
D E Y A D R O B A L V O H D
L L L S V E T E R A N S S A
A E S O J F P B S S L H U R
I C A L R L F E M I Y A B A
R T I U H A R O N E M K M P
O I N T T G C C K D W K U D
M O T H E R O R D A E U L A
E N E E T L U I N P A N O S
M R J R N T P Z W R R A C H
X T S U G U A G H I B H M E
X M A R C H E H P L O D U R
T A E R T R O K C I R T P G
```

Food Processor

Each sentence below contains the name of a food or drink hidden between two or more words. Underline each word as you find it and then circle it in the grid. Ignore spacing and punctuation. We did the first one for you.

1. HAND ME THE M<u>AP, PLE</u>ASE.
2. THEY WON THE SAMBA CONTEST.
3. HERE'S YOUR BAG, ELSIE.
4. HE PROMISED TO BE A NICE BOY.
5. THE BEE FLEW OUT THE WINDOW.
6. DO YOU REMEMBER RYAN?
7. IS YOUR CAB READY?
8. SHE CAN DYE HER HAIR.
9. IS THE PALACE REALLY HUGE?
10. WAKE ME IF I SHOULD OVERSLEEP.
11. THEY LIVE RIGHT NEAR YOU.
12. CAN YOU CONNECT A RED TRAILER?
13. PAPA STARTED TO JOG.
14. CHOP EACH PIECE OF WOOD CAREFULLY.
15. LOOK FOR ICE CUBES.
16. HE HAS A LADDER.
17. IT'S SO DARK IN HERE.
18. I AM SO UPSET.
19. SEE THE WASP IN THE CHAIR.
20. DON'T WASTE A KID'S TIME.
21. GIVE TOM A TOY.
22. IT'S YOUR TURN, I PRESUME.
23. THEY LOVE A LOT OF THINGS.

Answer on page 85.

```
L P E A C H P G D M E
V Y R R E B V E A L C
L I V E R E Z Q L E I
X T S T E A K P A L R
Y O H C A N I P S P A
D M F Z L N U A H P T
N A Q I R O G S L A C
A T E U S Z B T M D E
C O T R J H B A C O N
X F E E B A G E L S Y
```

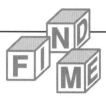

Music Maker

After you find 22 musical instruments, read the *leftover* letters from left to right and top to bottom to answer this riddle: Which storybook character wrote his own songs? Write the answer in the spaces at the bottom.

ACCORDION
BAGPIPE
BANJO
BASSOON
BELLS
CASTANETS
CELLO
CLARINET
DRUM
GUITAR
HARMONICA
HARP
KAZOO
KEYBOARD
MARIMBA
OBOE
ORGAN
PIANO
SAX
TRIANGLE
UKE
VIOLIN

K	A	C	I	N	O	M	R	A	H	B
A	E	K	U	A	L	G	X	R	C	E
Z	E	Y	A	G	L	U	A	A	L	L
O	P	O	B	R	E	I	S	G	A	L
O	I	P	N	O	C	T	N	M	R	S
V	P	H	J	A	A	A	A	U	I	V
A	G	N	A	N	I	R	N	R	N	I
O	A	W	E	R	I	P	D	D	E	O
B	B	T	T	M	P	I	N	K	T	L
O	S	L	B	A	S	S	O	O	N	I
E	E	A	C	C	O	R	D	I	O	N

Answer: __ __ __ __   __ __ __   __ __ __ __ __ __ __

Answer on page 95.

Tropical Games

After you find the 19 basketball terms, read the *leftover* letters from left to right and top to bottom to answer this riddle: How do people in Hawaii play basketball? Write the answer in the spaces at the bottom.

BASKET
CAGER
COURT
DEFENSE
DRIBBLE
DUNK
FEINT
FOUL
GUARD
JUMP
LAY-UP
LINE
N.B.A.
OFFENSE
POINT
REBOUND
SHOT
TIP-IN
WEAVE

C	R	E	B	O	U	N	D	D
O	B	A	S	K	E	T	R	E
U	W	H	F	I	K	I	A	F
R	O	T	O	N	B	E	U	E
T	F	H	U	B	V	J	G	N
N	F	D	L	A	Y	U	P	S
I	E	E	E	H	U	M	L	E
O	N	W	I	N	I	P	I	T
P	S	L	A	N	H	O	N	O
R	E	G	A	C	T	P	E	S

Answer: __ __ __ __ __ __ __ __ __ __ __ __ __

Answer on page 84.

Choices #2

Three words on each line look similar. Choose the one that matches the definition given and find only *that* word in the grid on the opposite page. Work back and forth between the grid and the word list if you're not sure of some definitions.

1. APPREHENDS - APPROVES - APPROACHES   Comes nearer
2. AQUA - AWKWARD - AMETHYST   Blue-green shade
3. AUDIENCE - AUDITION - AUCTION   A tryout by a performer
4. CLIQUE - CLIMATE - CLINIC   Hospital
5. CORRECT - CORDIAL - CORNY   Warm and friendly
6. DEFEND - DEFROST - DEFINE   Thaw out
7. EXHAUST - EXHALE - EXTEND   Breathe out
8. EXPENSE - EXPEDITION - EXPIRATION   A long trip
9. EXTINCT - EXTRAVAGANT - EXTREME   No longer living
10. GENUINE - GENTLE - GENEROUS   Not selfish
11. HOSTILE - HORRIBLE - HUSKY   Big and strong
12. INSIGNIA - INSOMNIA - INSERT   The inability to sleep
13. KHAKI - KARATE - KAYAK   Lightweight canoe
14. LADLE - LADDER - LADY   Large serving spoon
15. PASTEL - PASSION - PASSAGE   A strong feeling
16. PURPOSE - PORCUPINE - PORPOISE   Sea animal
17. PORTFOLIO - PORTRAIT - PORTION   Picture of a person
18. PYGMY - PYTHON - PUTTY   Very large snake
19. QUARTET - QUARTER - QUART   Group of four
20. SANDBOX - SANDPIPER - SANDBAR   A small bird
21. SPARSE - SUSPICIOUS - SPACIOUS   Roomy

Answer on page 85.

22. STRIVING - STRIDING - STRIKING   Attractive
23. TREACHEROUS - TRYING - TRENDY   Knowing the latest styles
24. UNWILLING - URGENT - UTMOST   Needing immediate action

```
A Q U A J Y N O I S S A P
C U H M L A D L E T S Q R
O A U Q E L A H X E A V Y
R R S U O I C A P S N T R
D T K A Y A K K E Y D N G
I E Y Z O C L L D N P N E
A T F R X W I N I G I O N
L Q P R U N E N T K P I E
Z P G P O R P O I S E T R
A M H H T S G R O L R I O
E X T I N C T E N B C D U
W Y V I N S O M N I A U S
P O R T R A I T N T G A M
```

Verbal Challenge #1

Don't look for the verbs listed here in the grid. Instead, look for a synonym of each word. For example, **QUARREL** is in the word list, but **ARGUE**, its synonym, is in the grid, and circled for you. Write the new words on the blank lines.

1. QUARREL _____ARGUE_____
2. BRAG _____
3. SCORCH _____
4. HEAL _____
5. SOAK _____
6. LAUGH _____
7. DESPISE _____
8. ASSIST _____
9. EXAMINE _____
10. PRESS _____
11. DEPART _____
12. HOBBLE _____
13. FIND _____
14. ADORE _____
15. LOSE _____
16. BEG _____
17. FLATTER _____
18. WANDER _____
19. PUSH _____
20. DOZE _____
21. DISINFECT _____
22. RIP _____
23. OBSERVE _____

L	P	R	A	I	S	E	E	I	E
P	E	O	L	N	L	T	V	R	Z
L	J	A	Q	S	E	A	O	O	I
E	X	M	V	P	E	C	H	N	L
A	R	G	U	E	P	O	S	I	I
D	W	A	T	C	H	L	M	H	R
B	O	A	S	T	Z	P	E	M	E
U	H	Q	D	R	E	N	C	H	T
R	M	I	S	P	L	A	C	E	S
N	G	I	G	G	L	E	R	U	C

Answer on page 87.

Code Breaker

Your mission is to decode a riddle and answer, and then find it in the grid. First, change each letter to the one that comes *immediately* before it in the alphabet. Write the real word (or words) on the blanks. Then find each word(s) in the grid. Note: If two words are on the same line, they will be found together in the grid.

I B W F _____

Z P V _____

I F B S E _____

B C P V U   U I F _____

F M F Q I B O U _____

X I P _____

X F O U _____

P O   B _____

D S B T I _____

E J F U   I F _____

X S F D L F E _____

B   C V T _____

U I S F F _____

D B S T _____

B O E   B _____

G J S F _____

F O H J O F _____

W	R	E	C	K	E	D	F	E
E	O	H	W	Y	Y	I	L	G
H	O	E	S	O	R	E	M	N
T	N	N	U	E	P	T	D	T
T	A	I	B	H	D	H	N	H
U	Z	G	A	E	S	E	T	R
O	X	N	S	A	H	A	V	E
B	T	E	S	R	A	C	R	E
A	M	A	N	D	A	L	K	C

Answer on page 94.

Play Ball

After you find the 24 baseball terms, read the *leftover* letters from left to right and top to bottom to finish this riddle: Why did the player on third base cry? Because he . . . Write the answer in the spaces at the bottom.

BALL
BATTER
BUNT
DOUBLE
FAN
FOUL
HELMET
INFIELD
INNING
MITT
MOUND
OUTFIELD
PITCHER
RUN
SHORTSTOP
SINGLE
SLIDE
STEAL
STRIKE
TEAM
THROW
UMPIRE
UNIFORM
WIND-UP

P	W	A	D	I	N	F	I	E	L	D
U	N	T	D	O	A	E	D	T	M	L
D	P	M	N	N	U	M	P	I	R	E
N	I	A	U	O	T	B	N	E	O	I
I	T	E	O	E	A	N	L	S	F	F
W	C	T	M	T	I	G	L	E	I	T
O	H	L	T	N	N	I	L	K	N	U
R	E	E	G	I	D	U	A	I	U	O
H	R	G	S	E	M	O	B	R	U	N
T	H	F	O	U	L	A	E	T	S	O
P	O	T	S	T	R	O	H	S	M	E

Answer: __

Answer on page 93.

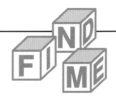

Off Course

After you find the 26 golfing terms, read the *leftover* letters from left to right and top to bottom to answer this riddle: What was the most famous golf game in American history? Write the answer in the spaces at the bottom.

BAG
BIRDIE
BOGEY
CADDIE
CART
CLUB
COURSE
DIVOT
DRIVER
EAGLE
FAIRWAY
GREEN
GRIP
HANDICAP
HAZARD
HOLE
IRON
PAR
PUTTER
ROUGH
SAND
SHOT
SLICE
SWING
WEDGE
WOOD

P	A	C	I	D	N	A	H	T	H	E
A	U	C	A	D	D	I	E	O	E	G
R	B	T	D	R	A	Z	A	H	L	D
E	O	S	T	T	B	O	G	E	Y	E
V	F	T	O	E	I	T	L	S	O	W
I	A	V	N	G	R	T	E	R	E	S
R	I	P	N	A	D	E	P	U	H	L
D	R	I	C	A	I	W	O	O	D	I
B	W	R	L	R	E	R	T	C	N	C
S	A	G	U	H	G	U	O	R	A	E
T	Y	G	B	G	R	E	E	N	S	Y

Answer: __ __ __ __ __ __ __ __ __ __ __ __ __ __ __ __

Answer on page 87.

Anagrams #2

Each word in the list can be anagrammed—its letters rearranged to form a new word. First, figure out the new word. (Use the starting letter we've provided as a hint.) Then, find each new word in the grid on the opposite page and circle it. Remember, in an anagram *all the letters* of the original word will be used. The first one is done for you.

1. MANGO	AMONG	12. STREAM	M_____
2. ASSUME	A_____	13. ASLEEP	P_____
3. MANILA	A_____	14. QUITE	Q_____
4. REPAID	D_____	15. SECURE	R_____
5. CREDIT	D_____	16. LUSTER	R_____
6. SQUEAL	E_____	17. TREASON	S_____
7. FAKER	F_____	18. RESIST	S_____
8. DANGER	G_____	19. PRIEST	S_____
9. MELONS	L_____	20. WASTE	S_____
10. RAMBLE	M_____	21. HATRED	T_____
11. CHARM	M_____	22. WARDEN	W_____

Answer on page 85.

```
R  E  Q  U  A  L  S  W  E  A  T
E  W  U  R  V  N  E  D  R  A  G
P  L  I  M  W  C (A  M  O  N  G)
A  S  E  N  A  T  O  R  O  A  S
I  T  T  B  N  R  M  X  R  N  I
D  R  P  R  D  R  B  E  P  I  S
I  I  H  T  E  Z  T  L  L  M  T
R  P  G  S  R  S  Q  V  E  A  E
E  E  U  M  A  R  C  H  A  L  R
C  L  Z  M  Y  A  M  U  S  E  S
T  H  R  E  A  D  F  R  E  A  K
```

Finish/Start

You can add the same word to each letter group to make the end of one word and the start of another word. Just take each 3-letter word from the box below and place it in the blank spaces on each line to finish one word and start another word. Cross off each word as you use it. Warning: The word you put into the blank space *must* work for both sets of letters. After you know which words you're looking for, circle them in the grid on the opposite page.

AGE	ANT	ARE	BAN
CAN	CAT	DEN	LET
MAL	MET	PAL	PET
ROT	THE	TOM	TON

1. A N I / _____ / T E D

2. B E W / _____ / N A S

3. B O B / _____ / T L E

4. B O T / _____ / A T O

5. C A R / _____ / A L S

6. C A R / _____ / G U E

7. G A R / _____ / T A L

8. H E L / _____ / H O D

9. M A N / _____ / N D A

10. O I L / _____ / D L E

11. P A R / _____ T E N

12. P E N / _____ / A C E

13. T A B / _____ / T E R

14. T E E / _____ / O R Y

15. T E N / _____ / L E R

16. T U R / _____ / I S H

Answer on page 85.

P	D	N	P	H	S	I	N	A	B	L	C	M	P
T	E	E	T	H	E	C	A	R	T	O	N	A	N
C	A	T	T	L	E	X	B	E	W	A	R	E	P
Z	A	N	T	L	E	R	R	R	B	R	T	A	E
D	O	I	L	C	A	N	U	O	O	C	L	Y	N
Q	E	J	X	R	N	M	T	T	B	A	E	S	P
D	R	N	E	N	I	M	G	T	C	R	U	N	A
B	C	N	T	G	M	B	A	E	A	P	G	E	L
M	A	H	R	A	A	B	D	N	T	E	N	D	T
S	X	J	E	Z	L	T	O	M	A	T	O	R	E
S	L	A	T	E	P	V	H	X	T	G	T	A	N
B	O	T	T	O	M	L	T	A	D	N	E	G	A
Y	R	O	E	H	T	P	E	L	D	N	A	C	N
W	H	Z	L	H	E	L	M	E	T	M	G	L	T

Animal Charm

After you find the 22 animals, read the *leftover* letters from left to right and top to bottom to answer this riddle: Why wasn't the baby goat punished when it played a joke on the farmer? Write the answer in the spaces at the bottom.

ANTELOPE
BEAR
BEAVER
BURRO
CHEETAH
DEER
DONKEY
HAMSTER
HARE
HOG
HYENA
KOALA
LLAMA
MOLE
MOUSE
OCELOT
RABBIT
TIGER
VOLE
WOLF
YAK
ZEBRA

G	O	H	A	M	S	T	E	R	R	M
K	K	O	A	L	A	I	T	E	O	W
A	B	A	S	T	J	U	G	U	S	O
Y	H	E	T	K	E	I	S	I	D	C
E	Y	F	A	N	T	E	L	O	P	E
K	E	L	O	V	D	B	H	I	N	L
N	N	O	L	G	E	M	A	C	A	O
O	A	W	R	A	O	R	R	U	B	T
D	E	E	R	L	M	O	E	U	N	D
A	R	B	E	Z	R	A	B	B	I	T

Answer: _ _ _ _ _ _ _ _ _

_ _ _ _ _ _ _ _ _ _ _ _

Answer on page 90.

Follow the Leader #2

Find a string of connected words in the grid. Start with **MOTHER** (which is circled for you) and then find a 6-letter word that starts with the **R** in **MOTHER**. After you find the second word, look for the third word. It starts with **D** and has five letters. The list below will guide you. Continue in this way until you've found the last word, which will be related to **MOTHER**.

1. M O T H E R
2. R _ _ _ _ _ _
3. D _ _ _ _ _
4. N _ _ _
5. N _ _ _ _ _ _ _
6. G _ _ _ _
7. H _ _ _ _
8. S _ _ _ _
9. M _ _ _ _ _ _
10. D _ _ _
11. G _ _ _ _ _ _
12. N _ _
13. W _ _ _
14. K _ _ _
15. E _ _ _ _
16. S _ _ _ _

17. R _ _
18. G _ _ _ _ _
19. N _ _ _ _ _ _

J	M	X	T	H	S	A	G	W	E
R	I	A	E	L	G	N	H	M	R
K	W	R	S	U	I	R	N	R	U
L	S	Y	R	H	Y	M	E	W	T
R	M	Z	T	U	E	Z	H	E	A
E	E	O	R	J	O	D	L	V	N
H	N	M	N	X	O	S	D	N	E
T	U	Z	I	G	O	L	D	E	N
O	O	Y	V	N	R	Y	N	K	O
M	N	E	Z	O	D	K	N	I	W

Answer on page 93.

First Names (He)

The last names of some famous men (both past and present) are listed below. Next to each name there's a short description of his claim to fame. Write each man's first name in the blank space and then find that name in the grid on the opposite page.

1. _____ Einstein (scientist who won a Nobel Prize in 1921)

2. _____ Franklin (inventor of electricity)

3. _____ Gates (Microsoft head, and one of the richest men in the world)

4. _____ Dickens (author of *Oliver Twist*)

5. _____ Boone (frontiersman)

6. _____ Crockett (frontiersman)

7. _____ Whitney (inventor of the cotton gin)

8. _____ Autry (the singing cowboy)

9. _____ Lendl (tennis player)

10. _____ Robinson (first African-American to play Major League baseball)

11. _____ Lennon (one of the Beatles)

12. _____ Neiman (painter of athletes)

13. _____ Carroll (author of *Alice in Wonderland*)

14. _____ Twain (pen name of Samuel L. Clemens, author of *Tom Sawyer*)

15. _____ Mandela (first black president of South Africa)

16. _____ Picasso (Spanish painter and sculptor)

17. _____ Revere (patriot who had a "midnight ride")

18. _____ Morse (inventor of the Morse code)

19. _____ Woods (professional golf player)

20. _____ Disney (creator of Mickey Mouse)

21. _____ Gagarin (first human to go into space)

Answer on page 94.

Z	J	B	L	T	I	G	E	R	L
E	L	I	Q	H	R	G	K	B	B
N	E	L	S	O	N	E	E	W	M
H	R	L	Y	M	S	N	B	A	J
O	O	L	B	A	P	E	R	L	J
J	Y	V	M	S	W	K	E	T	A
Q	Y	U	R	I	I	I	F	M	C
S	E	I	V	A	N	W	Z	Z	K
L	Y	C	H	A	R	L	E	S	I
Y	V	A	D	P	A	U	L	L	E

Adjective Adventure #1

Don't look for these listed adjectives in the grid. Instead, look for a synonym of each word. For example, **MAD** is in the word list, but **ANGRY**, its synonym, is in the grid, and circled for you. Write the new words on the blank lines.

1. MAD __ANGRY__
2. SHY _____
3. ADORABLE _____
4. ENTHUSIASTIC _____
5. BENDABLE _____
6. COLD _____
7. STUFFED _____
8. COMICAL _____
9. BAD-TEMPERED _____
10. ENORMOUS _____
11. ACTIVE _____
12. FAITHFUL _____
13. FORTUNATE _____

14. IDEAL _____
15. UNDECORATED _____
16. PREPARED _____
17. SKINNY _____
18. CHEAP _____
19. WEIRD _____
20. DUMB _____
21. NOT WILD _____
22. GRATEFUL _____
23. SMALL _____
24. DIFFERENT _____

Answer on page 87.

```
S  T  I  N  G  Y  Y  M  T  B  Y
Y  T  Q  X (Y  R  G  N  A) P  R
P  E  R  F  E  C  T  S  M  S  L
D  L  E  A  G  L  H  U  E  L  O
I  U  A  H  N  F  R  V  I  E  Y
G  N  D  I  U  G  D  V  L  N  A
I  I  Y  L  N  X  E  B  I  D  L
R  Q  P  H  B  L  I  T  Z  E  U
F  U  N  N  Y  X  E  Z  U  R  C
U  E  H  G  E  A  G  E  R  C  K
L  M  P  L  S  T  U  P  I  D  Y
L  U  F  K  N  A  H  T  H  Y  N
```

Found Letters #2

One letter was added to each word in the list before it was put into the grid. For example: **FILED** is in the list, the **A** was added, and **FAILED** was circled. Find all the *new* words, circle them, and write the added letter on the line. When you've found all the words, read the found letters from 1 to 22 to answer this riddle: What is black and white and has 16 wheels? Write the answer in the spaces at the bottom.

1. FILED _____
2. PRIES _____
3. HAVEN _____
4. TIMER _____
5. BEAD _____
6. PLACE _____
7. SEATS _____
8. NOSE _____
9. MISER _____
10. CARTS _____
11. FIGHT _____
12. CANE _____
13. SIP _____
14. SPARKED _____
15. PLANT _____
16. STEAM _____
17. PORT _____
18. WEE _____
19. GRIN _____
20. CLOSE _____
21. CRAM _____
22. OFTEN _____

E	C	A	L	A	P	H	S	C	F	S
S	M	S	P	O	R	T	L	A	P	P
I	R	E	T	S	I	M	I	N	L	A
O	M	Y	N	M	Z	L	P	O	A	R
N	A	T	B	H	E	A	V	E	N	K
E	E	E	G	D	S	H	V	W	E	L
T	R	S	T	R	A	H	C	E	T	E
F	T	O	S	T	A	E	W	S	H	D
O	S	L	T	H	G	I	R	F	M	J
S	T	C	R	E	A	M	N	B	Y	Q

Answer: __ __ __ __ __ __ __ __ __ __

__ __ __ __ __ __ __ __ __ __ __ __

Answer on page 92.

Tree-mendous Fun

ACACIA
ALDER
ASH
CEDAR
CHERRY
CYPRESS
EUCALYPTUS
GUAVA
HICKORY
OAK
OLIVE
PALM
PAPAYA
PINE
PLUM
POMEGRANATE
POPLAR
SEQUOIA
TANGERINE
TEAK
TULIP
WALNUT

After you find this list of 22 trees, read the *leftover* letters from left to right and top to bottom to answer this riddle: Why did the tree surgeon buy another office? Write the answer in the blanks at the bottom.

E	T	A	N	A	R	G	E	M	O	P
N	U	W	A	L	N	U	T	H	A	O
I	L	C	C	E	O	A	K	L	L	P
R	I	W	A	A	S	V	M	I	E	L
E	P	R	C	L	B	A	V	N	C	A
G	L	E	I	H	Y	E	I	R	Y	R
N	U	D	A	A	E	P	A	N	P	A
A	M	L	P	C	H	R	T	I	R	D
T	K	A	E	T	N	G	R	U	E	E
O	P	H	I	C	K	O	R	Y	S	C
U	H	S	A	I	O	U	Q	E	S	T

Answer: __ __   __ __ __

___ ___ ___ ___ ___ ___ ___ ___ ___ ___   ___ ___ ___

Answer on page 93.

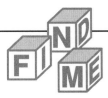

Hear Ye! #2

A homophone is a word that sounds just like another word but is spelled differently and has a different meaning. Look at each word in the list and find its homophone in the grid. For example, **BEAT** is listed, but **BEET** is in the grid. Write the new words on the blank lines.

1. BEAT ___BEET___

2. BOARD _____

3. DIE _____

4. AIR _____

5. LAX _____

6. MAID _____

7. KNIGHT _____

8. PAIL _____

9. PAIN _____

10. POLL _____

11. PRAYS _____

12. PRIDE _____

13. WRAPPER _____

14. WRY _____

15. SEIZE _____

16. SOARS _____

17. STAIRS _____

18. SUEDE _____

19. SUITE _____

20. VEIN _____

21. WAIVE _____

22. WHETHER _____

23. WEAK _____

24. WAY _____

25. WAIL _____

Answer on page 88.

G	H	P	M	G	S	K	C	A	L
T	P	R	H	W	B	O	R	E	D
H	G	I	E	W	H	Z	W	Y	E
G	S	E	I	Z	V	A	I	N	Y
I	T	D	R	R	V	C	L	B	A
N	A	V	R	E	H	T	A	E	W
M	R	E	R	P	S	O	R	E	S
A	E	M	L	P	O	L	E	T	C
D	S	S	E	A	S	K	E	Y	D
E	S	I	A	R	P	A	N	E	R

Body Language

Each sentence below contains the name of a part of the body hidden between two or more words. Underline each word as you find it and then circle it in the grid. Ignore spacing and punctuation. We did the first one for you.

1. THANK LEANN FOR THE PRESENT.
2. CEDAR MAY BE USED IN CLOSETS.
3. GRAB ONE BRASS RING.
4. PUT THE COBRA IN ITS CAGE.
5. WHICH ESTATE SHALL WE VISIT?
6. BUY LUNCH IN THE CAFETERIA.
7. THE ANGEL BOWED TO THE CHILDREN.
8. THE YELLING IS OVER.
9. TELL ME IF ACES ARE HIGH.
10. WE PLAYED GOLF IN GERMANY.
11. WATCH AND WAIT.
12. SHE ADDRESSED FOUR ENVELOPES.
13. THE ARTICLE IS IMPORTANT.
14. WHAT DOES CHUCK NEED?
15. THE GINGER ALE GOT WARM.
16. I AM OUT HERE.
17. WHAT DO RHINOS ENJOY?
18. THIS IS THE CAR I BOUGHT.
19. WHERE SHOULD ERIK GO?
20. WAS TOM A CHEERLEADER?

Answer on page 94.

21. WHAT HIGH SCHOOL DID YOU ATTEND?

22. DON'T HUM BEFORE BREAKFAST.

23. LET'S GO TO ENGLAND.

24. THEIR NAMES WERE ON THE BOSTON GUEST LIST.

25. DON'T LET HIM GET TOO THIRSTY.

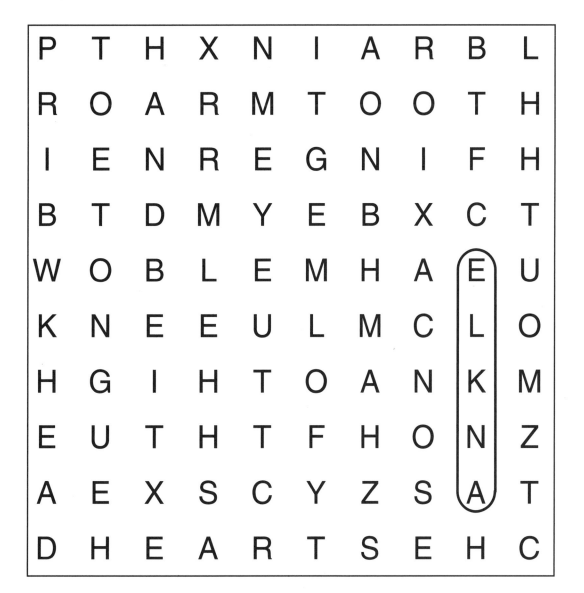

P	T	H	X	N	I	A	R	B	L
R	O	A	R	M	T	O	O	T	H
I	E	N	R	E	G	N	I	F	H
B	T	D	M	Y	E	B	X	C	T
W	O	B	L	E	M	H	A	E	U
K	N	E	E	U	L	M	C	L	O
H	G	I	H	T	O	A	N	K	M
E	U	T	H	T	F	H	O	N	Z
A	E	X	S	C	Y	Z	S	A	T
D	H	E	A	R	T	S	E	H	C

Hair and Bunny

The 35 random words below will all become weather words if you correctly change the boldfaced letter in each one. For example, change the **F** in **FRIGHT** to **B** and you have **BRIGHT**, which is circled in the grid on the opposite page. Find each *new* word, write it on the blank space, circle it in the grid, and then enjoy a FAIR and SUNNY day! Note: The bolded letter to be changed can be anywhere in the word.

1. **F**RIGHT   BRIGHT
2. **F**RISK _____
3. CHIL**D** _____
4. CLOU**T** _____
5. **B**OLD _____
6. **P**OOL _____
7. **L**AMP _____
8. **F**RIZZLE _____
9. **C**RY _____
10. **H**AIR _____
11. FO**R** _____
12. FROS**H** _____
13. **M**ALE _____
14. GUS**H** _____
15. **P**AIL _____
16. **L**AZY _____
17. **A**CE _____
18. **M**OLD _____

19. MIS**S** _____
20. **H**OIST _____
21. **B**UGGY _____
22. POU**T** _____
23. RAI**D** _____
24. SHA**K**Y _____
25. SL**O**WER _____
26. **F**LEET _____
27. SL**A**SH _____
28. SM**U**G _____
29. SNO**B** _____
30. ST**R**AY _____
31. ST**O**CKY _____
32. **B**UNNY _____
33. WAR**T** _____
34. **V**ET _____
35. W**A**ND _____

Answer on page 89.

```
L  W  E  T  S  L  H  G  H  F  M  Z
Y  A  Z  D  M  Q  O  A  Y  A  Q  W
A  R  A  V  O  F  Z  O  K  I  B  I
R  M  U  G  G  Y  R  D  C  R  X  N
P  P  O  U  R  M  K  S  I  R  B  D
S  M  M  I  S  T  Z  G  T  Y  U  R
N  F  R  O  S  T  H  J  S  O  C  I
X  I  Z  H  N  T  I  H  L  T  H  Z
E  L  A  G  O  E  R  C  S  B  I  Z
W  D  Z  R  W  E  O  U  E  U  L  L
Y  N  N  U  S  L  G  H  A  I  L  E
T  M  I  L  D  S  H  O  W  E  R  S
```

Number Code

Each letter in the alphabet was given a number, from 1 to 26. So, **A = 1**, **B = 2**, and ... **Z = 26**. Change each number below to its correct letter. Write the word or words on the line and then find each term in the grid to find a corny riddle. You can laugh or groan after you're done! Note: Words that are coded together will be found together in the grid.

23 8 1 20 _____

13 15 22 9 5 _____

20 5 12 12 19 _____

1 2 15 21 20   1 _____

16 18 5 20 20 25 _____

7 9 18 12 _____

23 8 15 _____

6 1 12 12 19 _____

9 14   12 15 22 5 _____

23 9 20 8 _____

1 14   21 7 12 25 _____

1 14 19 23 5 18 9 14 7 _____

13 1 3 8 9 14 5 _____

Answer on page 91.

" 2 5 1 21 20 25   _____

1 14 4   _____

20 8 5   _____

2 5 5 16 "   _____

A	B	O	U	T	A	T	W	P
N	N	S	L	L	A	F	E	E
D	H	S	Z	H	W	E	V	T
A	O	H	W	I	B	O	M	M
N	X	V	T	E	L	L	S	O
U	E	H	A	N	R	B	T	V
G	H	U	I	L	R	I	G	I
L	T	M	A	C	H	I	N	E
Y	T	T	E	R	P	P	Y	G

Synonym Search #2

Don't look for these listed words in the grid. Instead, look for a synonym of each word. For example, **OBSTACLE** is in the word list, but **BARRIER**, its synonym, is in the grid and circled for you. Write the new words on the blank lines.

1. OBSTACLE ___BARRIER___

2. MIDDLE _____

3. KID _____

4. JESTER _____

5. BROOK _____

6. PHYSICIAN _____

7. FOE _____

8. CLOTH _____

9. PAL _____

10. OIL _____

11. VISITOR _____

12. CORRIDOR _____

13. ATTORNEY _____

14. RACE _____

15. COUNTRY _____

16. GLUE _____

17. SELLER _____

18. PLAN _____

19. ODOR _____

20. SHOP _____

21. ROBBER _____

22. CEASEFIRE _____

23. DICTATOR _____

Answer on page 92.

P	F	E	I	H	T	J	L	G	B	S
M	A	E	D	Y	Z	L	V	U	A	T
A	Q	S	R	L	A	W	Y	E	R	O
R	E	A	T	H	I	N	X	S	R	R
A	N	E	Z	E	A	H	W	T	I	E
T	E	R	E	T	N	E	C	R	E	L
H	M	G	I	C	M	I	V	U	R	D
O	Y	O	L	E	R	O	T	C	O	D
N	N	O	H	B	Z	E	Y	E	Q	E
R	W	C	A	Z	S	M	E	L	L	P
N	S	F	R	I	E	N	D	K	H	Z

Slang Search

Okay, it's time to look for slang words used in everyday speech. Each sentence describes a slang term hidden on the opposite page. The first letter of each word is given, and spaces are left for the number of letters in the answer. (Sometimes there's a hint in parentheses.) Here's your chance to use your N - - - - - (see # 17).

1. Something that's a failure is a B - - - (nuclear explosion).
2. A foolish person is called a B - - - (he clowns around).
3. People standing in a row at a cafeteria make up a C - - -   L - - -.
4. Throw junk mail away in the C - - - - - - -   F - - - (wastebasket).
5. Someone who watches a lot of TV is a C - - - -   P - - - - - (sofa + spud).
6. Your nice clothing is called G - - -   R - - -.
7. Someone who runs errands in a company is a G - - - -.
8. A really neat thing is G - - - - - (really fab).
9. A detective is a G - - - - - - (think of his footwear).
10. When you're happy you're in H - -   H - - - - - (swine + the hereafter).
11. Another term for TV is I - - - -   B - - (stupid shape).
12. The primary street in a town is called the M - - -   D - - -.
13. A stupid person is called a M - - - - - - - (it's in spaghetti).
14. A person who talks and talks and talks is a M - - - -   M - - - -.
15. When you get hungry and want to eat junk food, you have the M - - - - - - - -.
16. A very short period of time is a N - -   Y - - -   M - - - - -
    (a large eastern city + 60 seconds).
17. When you think things out, you are using your N O O D L E.
18. To heat up food in the microwave you N - - - it (blast it).
19. A Western (movie) is called an O - - - - (horse food).
20. A very thick fog is P - -   S - - - (something you eat with a spoon).
21. When you eat and eat and eat some more, you P - -   O - -.
22. A dog is a P - - - - (rhymes with "mooch").
23. The head of a company or the country is the P - - - -.
24. A convertible car is called a R - -   T - - (the part that folds down).
25. The overnight flight from Los Angeles to New York is the R - - - - -.

Answer on page 92.

26. A bad hairpiece is called a R - - (you want to step on it).

27. When you want to sleep you're trying to get some S - - - - - -
(the same body part as #25).

28. Someone who isn't realistic and seems to be from another planet
is a S - - - -   C - - - -.

29. Something bad is a T - - - - - (Thanksgiving bird).

30. A quarter isn't worth much, only about T - -   B - - -.

31. A stupid person is a Y - - - - (a toy that goes up and down).

32. No! You won't eat it because it's just plain Y - - - -.

33. But something that tastes delicious is Y - - - -.

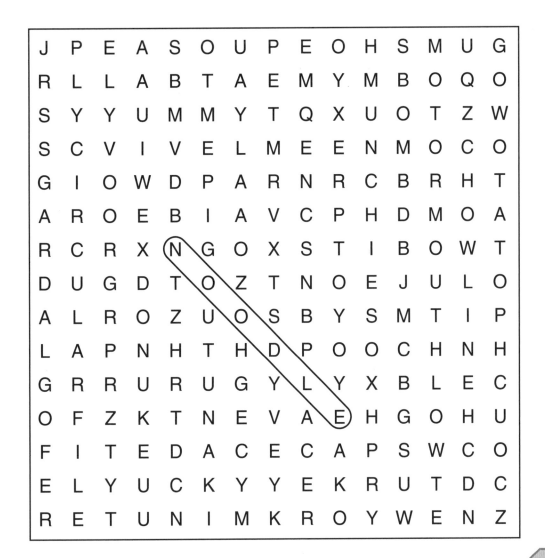

```
J  P  E  A  S  O  U  P  E  O  H  S  M  U  G
R  L  L  A  B  T  A  E  M  Y  M  B  O  Q  O
S  Y  Y  U  M  M  Y  T  Q  X  U  O  T  Z  W
S  C  V  I  V  E  L  M  E  E  N  M  O  C  O
G  I  O  W  D  P  A  R  N  R  C  B  R  H  T
A  R  O  E  B  I  A  V  C  P  H  D  M  O  A
R  C  R  X  N  G  O  X  S  T  I  B  O  W  T
D  U  G  D  T  O  Z  T  N  O  E  J  U  L  O
A  L  R  O  Z  U  O  S  B  Y  S  M  T  I  P
L  A  P  N  H  T  H  D  P  O  O  C  H  N  H
G  R  R  U  R  U  G  Y  L  Y  X  B  L  E  C
O  F  Z  K  T  N  E  V  A  E  H  G  O  H  U
F  I  T  E  D  A  C  E  C  A  P  S  W  C  O
E  L  Y  U  C  K  Y  Y  E  K  R  U  T  D  C
R  E  T  U  N  I  M  K  R  O  Y  W  E  N  Z
```

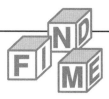

Follow the Leader #3

Find a string of connected words in the grid. Start with **BACK** (which is circled for you) and then find a 3-letter word that starts with the **K** in **BACK**. After you find the second word, look for the third word. It starts with **T** and has four letters. The list below will guide you. Continue in this way until you've found the last word, which will be related to **BACK**.

1. B A C K
2. K _ _ _
3. T _ _ _ _
4. L _ _ _ _
5. D _ _ _ _
6. T _ _ _
7. O _ _ _ _
8. Y _ _ _ _
9. R _ _ _ _
10. H _ _ _ _
11. D _ _ _ _
12. K _ _ _ _ _
13. D _ _ _ _
14. W _ _ _
15. O _ _ _ _
16. R _ _ _
17. D _ _ _ _ _
18. Y _ _ _ _
19. P _ _ _ _

V	Y	X	Y	Y	Y	E	L	P	M
Y	W	L	J	E	R	Z	L	A	Q
M	N	G	N	H	A	L	P	C	Y
O	W	T	H	C	I	R	T	K	R
P	W	R	S	E	D	E	R	G	M
N	M	Z	Q	U	A	X	E	V	N
K	I	T	B	J	D	D	V	M	D
C	M	E	Y	N	R	E	O	N	R
A	B	L	A	S	C	S	I	H	E
B	L	L	N	Y	G	K	N	Y	W

Answer on page 89.

Dog Daze

After you find the dog breeds, read the *leftover* letters from left to right and top to bottom to answer this riddle: What is a dog's favorite food? Write the answer in the spaces at the bottom.

ALSATIAN
BOXER
BULLDOG
CHOW
COLLIE
DACHSHUND
DOBERMAN
GREYHOUND
HUSKY
MALAMUTE
MUTT
PUG
PULI
SAMOYED
SETTER
TERRIER

D	G	A	A	C	H	O	W	M	D
T	E	U	L	B	O	E	A	N	R
E	A	Y	P	S	G	L	U	L	E
R	E	U	O	B	A	H	L	G	T
R	L	H	O	M	S	T	O	I	T
I	W	X	U	H	A	D	I	T	E
E	E	T	C	S	L	S	U	A	S
R	E	A	I	L	K	M	T	H	N
L	D	N	U	O	H	Y	E	R	G
D	O	B	E	R	M	A	N	O	X

Answer: __ __ __ __ __ __ __ __ __ __ __ __

Answer on page 95.

Adjective Adventure #2

Don't look for these listed adjectives in the grid. Instead, look for a synonym of each word. For example, **COLD** is in the word list, but **CHILLY**, its synonym, is in the grid and circled for you. Write the new words on the blank lines

1. COLD ____CHILLY____

2. UNCHANGING _____

3. EXPENSIVE _____

4. UNLIT _____

5. EXTREME _____

6. OLD _____

7. THRILLED _____

8. PRIMARY _____

9. OILY _____

10. SUPER! _____

11. HAPPY _____

12. TARDY _____

13. SMALLEST _____

14. INSIGNIFICANT _____

15. SCARCE _____

16. NORMAL _____

17. UNMOVING _____

18. REALLY _____

19. RANDOM _____

20. FALSE _____

Answer on page 91.

68

```
Z J C O S T L Y Z E
D E N N A L P N U X
R R X E C V S R M C
A E R L T H T Y J I
S G G D R N I O G T
T U R E U R L L X E
I L E R L L L A L D
C A A L Y P E T T Y
W R S Y M K R A D E
E N Y H B F I R S T
S G C O N S T A N T
```

Clothes Encounters

After you find 18 things to wear, read the *leftover* letters from left to right and top to bottom to answer this riddle: What kind of clothing did Cinderella wear? Write the answer in the spaces at the bottom.

COAT
COSTUME
HAT
JACKET
JEANS
JUMPER
KILT
PANTS
PULLOVER
ROBE
SHIRT
SHORTS
SLACKS
SWEATER
TIE
TURTLENECK
TUXEDO
VEST

S	N	A	E	J	A	C	K	E	T
H	L	P	W	I	H	A	T	U	U
O	E	A	U	S	H	I	R	T	X
R	M	S	C	L	E	T	H	A	E
T	U	R	N	K	L	C	S	D	D
S	T	O	W	E	S	O	E	E	O
T	S	B	N	A	T	A	V	R	V
L	O	E	C	L	N	T	O	E	T
I	C	S	W	E	A	T	E	R	R
K	H	J	U	M	P	E	R	E	S

Answer: __

Answer on page 95.

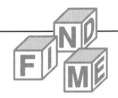

Yummy!

After you find 17 desserts, read the *leftover* letters from left to right and top to bottom to answer this riddle: What is a mouse's favorite dessert? Write the answer in the spaces at the bottom.

BAKLAVA
BROWNIE
COOKIE
CREAM PUFF
CREPE
CUSTARD
ECLAIR
FLAN
FRAPPE
FRUIT
ICE CREAM
JELLO
MACAROON
OATMEAL BAR
PARFAIT
PIE
TRIFLE

M	A	C	A	R	O	O	N	F	R
B	A	K	L	A	V	A	C	F	A
H	F	E	J	E	L	L	O	U	B
P	R	P	R	F	P	E	C	P	L
A	U	P	E	C	I	S	O	M	A
R	I	A	L	C	E	E	O	A	E
F	T	R	C	P	A	C	K	E	M
A	K	F	E	E	L	F	I	R	T
I	B	R	O	W	N	I	E	C	A
T	C	U	S	T	A	R	D	E	O

Answer: __ __ __ __ __ __ __ __ __ __ __

Answer on page 95.

Rhyme Time

In this weak diversion, or "lame game," the answer to each clue is a pair of words that rhyme with each other. First, figure out the two-word nonsense phrase that answers each clue. To help you out, the first letter of each answer word is given, nd the blanks tell you how many letters are in each word. Next, find each phrase in the grid on the opposite page. We've done the first one for you. Give a #21 when you're finished!

1. Crooked camping "home"   BENT   TENT
2. Favorite examination   B - - -   T - - -
3. Large animal that lives in a sty B - -   P - -
4. Smart lamp   B - - - - -   L - - - -
5. Chilly swimming spot   C - - -   P - - -
6. Adorable musical instrument   C - - -   F - - - -
7. Honest couple   F - - -   P - - -
8. Phony leaf-collecting tool   F - - -   R - - -
9. Chubby kitten   F - -   C - -
10. Healthy Christmas tree   F - - -   P - - -
11. Enjoyable race   F - -   R - -
12. Tardy husband or wife   L - - -   M - - -
13. Principal choo-choo   M - - -   T - - - -
14. Pastel-colored basin   P - - -   S - - -
15. Faster chooser   Q - - - - - -   P - - - - -
16. Genuine hog sound   R - - -   S - - - - -
17. Bright-colored sleeping place   R - -   B - -
18. Gloomy boy   S - -   L - -
19. Identical picture holder   S - - -   F - - - -
20. Bashful man   S - -   G - -

Answer on page 89.

21. Great shout   S - - - -   Y - - - -
22. High shopping center   T - - -   M - - -
23. Skinny leg part   T - - -   S - - -
24. Very tiny buzzing insect   W - -   B - -
25. Damp plane   W - -   J - -

```
R E K C I P R E K C I U Q N X
I S P Y Y R G T H I N S H I N
A N H N F I N E P I N E Q A Z
P G Y Y P W L J B F Z R L R T
R M P G G H R T Q V A X M T H
I L I Y C U T E F L U T E N G
A B N X L W Y W A Z W A C I I
F A K E R A K E D B E L O A L
U P S T R X U A N E E L O M T
N D I S M Q L H L S B M L N H
R E N Q S D M G R T E A P Y G
U B K L A T E M A T E L O C I
N D A S W E L L Y E L L O Z R
W E M A R F E M A S B Q L W B
R R V P G L B E N T T E N T M
```

Capital Fun

Don't go to any of the state capitals on this list, because they're all scrambled into nonsense phrases. However, you can visit them after you do four things: 1) unscramble each phrase; 2) write the "real" capital city on the blank space; 3) locate it in the grid; 4) circle it. It's okay to use an atlas. The first one is done for you. Remember: A city name can be two words!

1. LAB NAY __ALBANY__

2. TAT LANA _____

3. IN US AT _____

4. I BE SO _____

5. TO SNOB _____

6. HENNY CEE _____

7. SUM LO CUB _____

8. RED VEN _____

9. REV DO _____

10. TANK OFF RR _____

11. LEAN HE _____

12. LOON HULU _____

13. U JANE U _____

14. TOM LINE REP _____

15. VANES HILL _____

16. NO PIX HE _____

17. RE RIPE _____

18. DIVER COP EN _____

19. LEG HAIR _____

20. CHIN DORM _____

21. NOT AS CREAM _____

22. ME LAS _____

23. SAFE NAT _____

24. GEL FIND RIPS _____

25. UP LAST _____

26. POKE AT _____

27. RENT NOT _____

Answer on page 93.

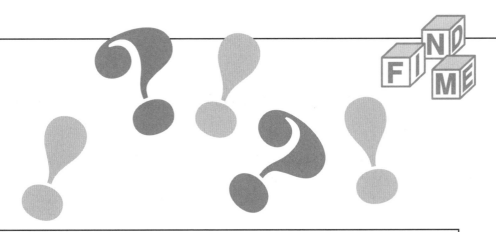

```
N A T N A L T A N E L E H J S
H S W D L H O N O L U L U R L
Z P F O F R P P H O E N I X M
P R O V I D E N C E E C S N O
T I C E Y C K N D A H R C H N
C N M R Y N A B U M T S L R T
H G S U B M U L O C N L F T P
E F A T N A S N B P I E R R E
Y I N U S L D O R A H E A A L
E E T P S T S E W S N N N L I
N L V A B T P Y N T G Y K E E
N D L C O T I A O V T N F I R
E E T N I L N N U H E V O G R
M L N A S H V I L L E R R H M
K O T N E M A R C A S N T T C
```

Unlisted "B" Words

Here's a puzzle without a word list. Your mission is to find 24 nouns that start with the letter **B**. Write your words on the blank spaces and check your list with ours in the answer section.

1. _____

2. _____

3. _____

4. _____

5. _____

6. _____

7. _____

8. _____

9. _____

10. _____

11. _____

12. _____

B	A	B	O	O	N	B	O	A	T
B	A	S	K	E	T	B	X	H	S
W	V	B	R	A	C	E	C	Y	A
M	N	L	Y	J	B	A	R	G	E
B	L	I	S	T	E	R	Z	B	B
A	L	Z	T	L	E	B	L	U	A
D	A	Z	B	B	T	W	S	R	N
G	B	A	L	C	O	N	Y	E	A
E	A	R	Z	B	A	R	N	A	N
Q	Y	D	R	A	O	B	L	U	A

13. _____

14. _____

15. _____

16. _____

17. _____

18. _____

19. _____

20. _____

21. _____

22. _____

23. _____

24. _____

Answer on page 91.

Verbal Challenge #2

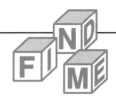

Don't look for the verbs listed here in the grid. Instead, look for a synonym of each word. For example, **ACCOMPLISH** is in the word list, but **ACHIEVE**, its synonym, is in the grid and circled for you. Write the new words on the blank lines.

1. ACCOMPLISH   ACHIEVE
2. CONSENT _____
3. ANNOY _____
4. SHATTER _____
5. PICK _____
6. POSTPONE _____
7. SADDEN _____
8. CONTRIBUTE _____
9. LENGTHEN _____
10. CONCEAL _____
11. RUSH _____
12. THAW _____
13. REPAIR _____
14. COPY _____
15. SWEAT _____
16. PRINT _____
17. PENALIZE _____
18. BUY _____
19. RESIGN _____
20. STAND _____
21. REMAIN _____
22. DISAPPEAR _____

B	R	E	A	K	E	L	T	L	E	M
M	O	Z	M	E	N	D	H	T	T	V
P	B	T	R	H	E	V	A	I	Q	P
E	H	G	H	S	I	N	U	P	D	U
S	A	U	O	E	O	Q	Z	E	E	B
A	C	O	R	D	R	Z	L	R	P	L
H	H	M	J	R	W	A	W	S	R	I
C	I	I	Q	I	Y	Z	T	P	E	S
R	E	M	D	S	V	A	N	I	S	H
U	V	I	Y	E	Y	G	R	R	S	T
P	E	C	D	N	E	T	X	E	M	L

Answer on page 86.

Choices #3

Three words on each line look similar. Choose the one that matches the definition given and find only that word in the grid on the opposite page. Work back and forth between the grid and the word list if you're not sure of some definitions.

1. BARRACUDA - BARRICADE - BAROMETER   Fish with sharp teeth
2. CHAPLAIN - CHAP - CHAPEL   Small church
3. CHARITY - CHARIOT - CHARCOAL   Two-wheeled horse cart
4. COMMENT - COMMERCE - COMMA   Remark
5. CONCLUSION - CONCESSION
    - CONCENTRATION   Close attention
6. COURTEOUS - COURAGEOUS
    - COWARDLY   Polite towards others
7. CUNNING - CULTURED - CURIOUS   Interested in everything
8. DEVOTE - DEVOUR - DIVIDE   Eat in a greedy way
9. EMBER - EMERGENCY - EMERALD   Valuable green gem
10. EVADE - EVOLVE - EVICT   Force someone out of a place
11. FANTASY - FANATIC - FASHION   Something imaginary
12. GENIE - GENIUS - GENE   Brilliant person
13. HOMESICK - HOMEMADE - HOMELY   Unattractive
14. HUMANE - HUMID - HUMBLE   Modest
15. MAZE - MANGER - MAIZE   Corn plant
16. MANNER - MANUAL - MANTLE   Instruction book
17. MIDDLE - MUDDLE - MEDDLE   Interfere
18. MIGRANT - MILEAGE - MIDGET   Very small person
19. NIGHTINGALE - NIGHTMARE
    - NIGHTGOWN   Frightening dream
20. OBTUSE - OBSTINATE - OBESE   Very fat

Answer on page 95.

21. ORCHID - ORCHARD - ORCHESTRA   Delicate flower
22. PEDAL - PEDDLE - PUDDLE   Sell
23. PLATTER - PLATOON - PLATFORM   Large serving dish
24. QUIBBLE - QUAIL - QUAKE   Tremble
25. REGRET - REIGN - REJECT   Feel sorry about something
26. STAGE - STUMBLE - STAGGER   Move in an unsteady way
27. TORSO - TORNADO - TORTILLA   Wind storm with a funnel-shaped cloud

```
N  T  R  W  O  D  A  N  R  O  T  B  E  S
O  I  E  C  F  L  E  S  L  E  X  A  L  U
I  Z  G  H  A  A  W  V  G  E  Q  R  B  O
T  P  R  H  N  R  H  D  O  J  P  R  M  I
A  S  E  O  T  E  I  B  P  U  Z  A  U  R
R  U  T  M  A  M  A  I  Z  E  R  C  H  U
T  O  B  E  S  E  A  B  R  Y  D  U  G  C
N  E  Y  L  Y  T  O  R  C  H  I  D  H  E
E  T  K  Y  A  S  A  R  E  T  T  A  L  P
C  R  Z  A  R  U  V  G  Y  D  R  D  M  E
N  U  T  S  U  I  N  E  G  I  D  N  L  G
O  O  S  Q  L  Q  R  A  O  E  V  I  C  T
C  C  O  M  M  E  N  T  M  Y  R  T  H  Y
```

Best Quest #2

Check out your rhyming skills again. For each word in the list, there is a word that rhymes with it hidden in the grid. For example, **SCREECH** is listed, but **BEACH** is in the grid. In this puzzle, each hidden word has a different ending than the word in the list. Write the new words on the blank lines.

1. SCREECH ___BEACH___
2. FADE _____
3. WORK _____
4. EIGHTEEN _____
5. FOUL _____
6. FROZE _____
7. ROLLER _____
8. SHORTS _____
9. CLEAN _____
10. TIGHT _____
11. CANOPY _____
12. DIET _____
13. FOUR _____
14. STUFF _____
15. CONCERT _____
16. CONCEIT _____
17. BREEZE _____
18. REEF _____
19. LYNX _____
20. LEAK _____

```
N  M  G  D  B  R  A  I  D  R
E  Z  A  C  L  E  R  K  A  Z
E  E  S  J  G  C  A  L  Q  M
U  S  O  S  P  I  O  C  B  T
Q  O  L  S  W  P  R  H  H  H
U  N  I  Q  U  E  G  I  O  I
A  L  N  U  T  U  E  Y  W  N
R  T  E  I  O  F  G  T  L  K
T  R  U  R  I  O  T  L  V  S
Z  Q  M  T  H  E  S  E  K  C
```

Answer on page 93.

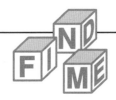

Spaced Out

After you find 21 words or terms related to outer space, read the *leftover* letters from left to right and top to bottom to finish this riddle: Why did the alien take soap into space with him? In case he ... Write the answer in the blanks at the bottom.

ARIES
COMET
EARTH
GALAXY
JUPITER
LYRA
MARS
MERCURY
MILKY WAY
MOON
NEBULA
NEPTUNE
NOVA
PLANET
PLUTO
SATELLITE
SATURN
STAR
SUNSPOT
URANUS
VENUS

R	C	N	E	N	U	T	P	E	N	A
E	S	O	V	A	T	E	N	A	L	P
T	E	V	M	E	R	C	U	R	Y	N
I	I	A	I	E	N	Y	N	T	T	Y
L	R	O	A	E	T	U	L	H	M	A
L	A	E	B	S	R	E	S	M	T	W
E	E	U	T	A	G	A	L	A	X	Y
T	L	A	N	I	T	N	O	R	R	K
A	R	U	S	U	P	H	O	S	O	L
S	S	W	R	P	L	U	T	O	E	I
S	U	N	S	P	O	T	J	R	M	M

Answer: __ __ __ __ __ __ __ __ __ __ __ __ __ __ __

__ __ __ __ __ __ __

Answer on page 90.

School Daze

After you find 17 school periods, read the *leftover* letters from left to right and top to bottom to answer this riddle: Why did the snakes have to stay after school? Write the answer in the blanks at the bottom.

ART
DRAMA
ETHICS
GEOGRAPHY
GRAMMAR
GYM
HEALTH
HISTORY
LUNCH
MATH
MUSIC
POETRY
READING
RECESS
SCIENCE
SPEECH
SPELLING

T	M	H	G	R	A	M	M	A	R
Y	E	A	D	R	A	M	A	Y	E
H	I	S	T	O	R	Y	Y	R	T
P	H	I	M	H	E	A	L	T	H
A	S	Y	S	E	C	D	R	E	I
R	G	N	I	D	A	E	R	O	C
G	T	L	U	N	C	H	E	P	S
O	E	C	N	E	I	C	S	P	H
E	M	U	S	I	C	E	B	U	S
G	S	S	P	E	L	L	I	N	G

Answer: __ __ __ __ __   __ __ __ __ __ __ __   __ __ __ __ __

Answer on page 93.

Missing Letters #2

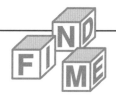

One letter was removed from each word in the list before it was put into the grid. Example: **PURSE** is in the list, the **S** was removed, and **PURE** was circled. Find all the new words, circle them, and write the missing letter on the line. When you've found all the words, read the missing letters from 1 to 16 to answer this riddle: What is a cannibal's favorite game? Write the answer on the blanks at the bottom.

1. PURSE __S__
2. SWINGING _____
3. HAUNTED _____
4. WORLDS _____
5. SHOVELS _____
6. LOOSER ____
7. WEIGHT _____
8. STARTS _____
9. THANKS ___
10. HEATS _____
11. FLIGHT _____
12. CREATE _____
13. HURRAY _____
14. FINDER _____
15. PLANETS ____
16. CRAVE ____

```
E  S  H  O  V  E  S  G  S
F  I  G  H  T  T  V  N  T
I  B  G  A  A  H  S  W  R
N  E  R  H  H  U  R  R  Y
E  C  V  S  T  N  A  L  P
R  J  W  A  V  T  T  O  U
M  Z  N  X  C  E  S  S  R
H  K  W  O  R  D  S  E  E
S  I  N  G  I  N  G  R  L
```

Answer: __ __ __ __ __ __ __   __ __ __   __ __ __ __ __ __ __

Answer on page 90.

Answers

Insect Aside

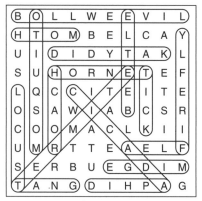

Answer: Because it was a litterbug.

Birds of a Feather

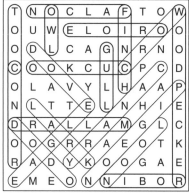

Answer: "Toucan play at that game."

Opposite Distraction

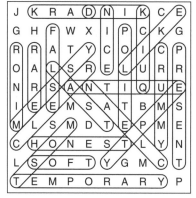

1. Antique	12. Messy
2. Clean	13. Minor
3. Clear	14. Most
4. Crummy	15. Nice
5. Dark	16. Polite
6. Empty	17. Present
7. False	18. Quick
8. Honest	19. Rare
9. Kind	20. Soft
10. Last	21. Temporary
11. Like	

Tropical Games

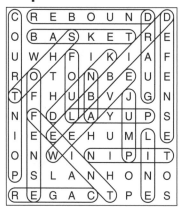

Answer: With hula hoops

Hear Ye! #1

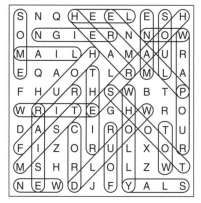

1. Cord
2. Fair
3. Four
4. Hear
5. Heel
6. Hoarse
7. Hour
8. Mail
9. Mane
10. Mist
11. New
12. Plane
13. Pour
14. Raise
15. Reign
16. Shoot
17. Slay
18. Some
19. Soul
20. Their
21. Tow
22. Wholly
23. Won
24. Would
25. Wrap
26. Write

Choices #2

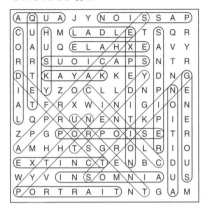

1. Approaches
2. Aqua
3. Audition
4. Clinic
5. Cordial
6. Defrost
7. Exhale
8. Expedition
9. Extinct
10. Generous
11. Husky
12. Insomnia
13. Kayak
14. Ladle
15. Passion
16. Porpoise
17. Portrait
18. Python
19. Quartet
20. Sandpiper
21. Spacious
22. Striking
23. Trendy
24. Urgent

Finish/Start

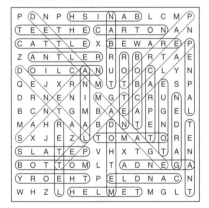

1. Animal/malted
2. Beware/arenas
3. Bobcat/cattle
4. Bottom/tomato
5. Carpet/petals
6. Carton/tongue
7. Garden/dental
8. Helmet/method
9. Manage/agenda
10. Oilcan/candle
11. Parrot/rotten
12. Penpal/palace
13. Tablet/letter
14. Teethe/theory
15. Tenant/antler
16. Turban/banish

Anagrams #2

1. Among
2. Amuses
3. Animal
4. Diaper
5. Direct
6. Equals
7. Freak
8. Garden
9. Lemons
10. Marble
11. March
12. Master
13. Please
14. Quiet
15. Rescue
16. Result
17. Senator
18. Sister
19. Stripe
20. Sweat
21. Thread
22. Wander

Food Processor

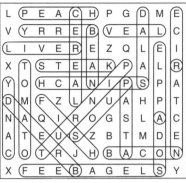

1. HAND ME THE <u>MAP, PLEASE</u>.
2. THEY WON THE SAM<u>BA CON</u>TEST.
3. HERE'S YOUR <u>BAG, ELSIE</u>.
4. HE PROMISED TO <u>BE A N</u>ICE BOY.
5. THE <u>BEE FLEW</u> OUT THE WINDOW.
6. DO YOU REMEM<u>BER RY</u>AN?
7. IS YOUR <u>CAB READY</u>?
8. SHE <u>CAN DYE</u> HER HAIR.
9. IS THE PALA<u>CE REAL</u>LY HUGE?
10. WAKE ME <u>IF I SHOULD</u> OVERSLEEP.
11. THEY <u>LIVE R</u>IGHT NEAR YOU.
12. CAN YOU CON<u>NECT A RED</u> TRAILER?
13. PA<u>PA STARTED</u> TO JOG.
14. CHOP <u>EACH</u> PIECE OF WOOD CAREFULLY.
15. LOOK FO<u>R ICE</u> CUBES.
16. HE HA<u>S A LADDER</u>.
17. IT'S <u>SO DARK</u> IN HERE.
18. I AM <u>SO UPSET</u>.
19. SEE THE WA<u>SP IN A CHAIR</u>.
20. DON'T WA<u>STE A KID</u>'S TIME.
21. GIVE <u>TOM A TOY</u>.
22. IT'S YOUR <u>TURN, I</u> PRESUME.
23. THEY LO<u>VE A LOT</u> OF THINGS.

Found Letters #1

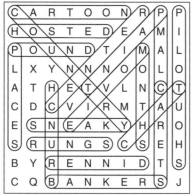

1. Country — R
2. Movie — I
3. Bankers — N
4. Rungs — G
5. Paint — A
6. Brunch — R
7. Cartoon — O
8. Pound — U
9. Months — N
10. Dinner — D
11. Hosted — T
12. Chat — H
13. Carets — E
14. Center — C
15. Shout — O
16. Clamp — L
17. Places — L
18. Pilot — I
19. Sneaky — E

Answer: . . . ring around the collie.

Anagrams #1

1. Bats
2. Clam
3. Course
4. Grate
5. Heart
6. Large
7. Leader
8. Lovely
9. Never
10. Pest
11. Remain
12. Shoe
13. Silent
14. Skater
15. Sour
16. Stain
17. Steal
18. Stride
19. Taxes
20. These
21. Throne
22. Throw
23. Trace

Verbal Challange #2

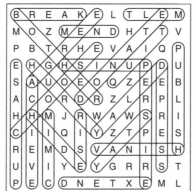

1. Achieve
2. Agree
3. Bother
4. Break
5. Choose
6. Delay
7. Depress
8. Donate
9. Extend
10. Hide
11. Hurry
12. Melt
13. Mend
14. Mimic
15. Perspire
16. Publish
17. Punish
18. Purchase
19. Quit
20. Rise
21. Stay
22. Vanish

First Names (She)

1. Amelia
2. Anne
3. Betsy
4. Chelsea
5. Clara
6. Diana
7. Drew
8. Emily
9. Georgia
10. Helen
11. Janet
12. Marie
13. Martha
14. Mary
15. Mia
16. Molly
17. Oprah
18. Rachel
19. Rosa
20. Sally
21. Tara
22. Venus

Adjective Adventure #1

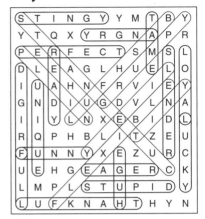

1. Angry
2. Bashful
3. Cute
4. Eager
5. Flexible
6. Frigid
7. Full
8. Funny
9. Grumpy
10. Huge
11. Lively
12. Loyal
13. Lucky
14. Perfect
15. Plain
16. Ready
17. Slender
18. Stingy
19. Strange
21. Stupid
21. Tame
22. Thankful
23. Tiny
24. Unique

Central Station

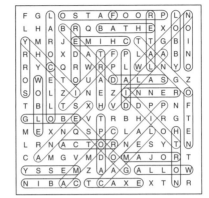

1. Actor/Order
2. Annex/Exact
3. Bathe/Heart
4. Cabin/Inner
5. Camel/ Elbow
6. Cello/Lobby
7. Chime/Messy
8. Comma/Major
9. Coral/Allow
10. Fatso/Sorry
11. Fruit/Itchy
12. Globe/Beard
13. Piano/North
14. Plaid/Idiot
15. Proof/Often
16. Salad/Adopt
17. Tango/Goose
18. Villa/Later
19. Wagon/Onion

Verbal Challenge #1

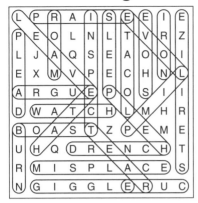

1. Argue
2. Boast
3. Burn
4. Cure
5. Drench
6. Giggle
7. Hate
8. Help
9. Inspect
10. Iron
11. Leave
12. Limp
13. Locate
14. Love
15. Misplace
16. Plead
17. Praise
18. Roam
19. Shove
20. Sleep
21. Sterilize
22. Tear
23. Watch

Off Course

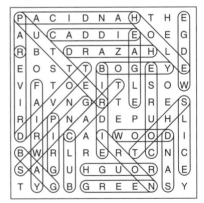

Answer: The Boston Tee Party.

Hear Ye! #2

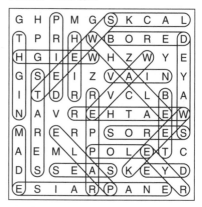

1. Beet
2. Bored
3. Dye
4. Heir
5. Lacks
6. Made
7. Night
8. Pale
9. Pane
10. Pole
11. Praise
12. Pried
13. Rapper
14. Rye
15. Seas
16. Sores
17. Stares
18. Swayed
19. Sweet
20. Vain
21. Wave
22. Weather
23. Week
24. Weigh
25. Whale

Flower Power

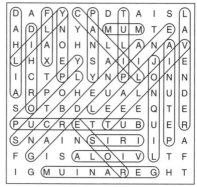

Answer: A daisy that has been in a fist fight.

Choices #1

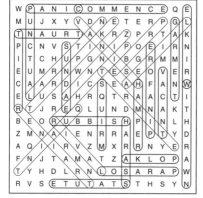

1. Aerial
2. Commence
3. Garment
4. Hamper
5. Harass
6. Natural
7. Panic
8. Parasol
9. Pinafore
10. Pitcher
11. Polka
12. Probe
13. Punctual
14. Quaint
15. Receipt
16. Rival
17. Rubbish
18. Squirm
19. Statute
20. Sundae
21. Termite
22. Trainer
23. Truant
24. Turnpike
25. Vacant
26. Vanish
27. Withdrawn
28. Wrinkle
29. Zinnia

Synonym Search #1

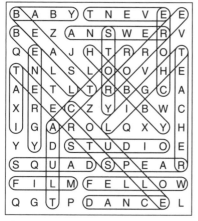

1. Actor
2. Adult
3. Answer
4. Baby
5. Beast
6. Bell
7. Chore
8. Couple
9. Dance
10. Energy
11. Error
12. Event
13. Fellow
14. Film
15. Hobby
16. Light
17. Spear
18. Squad
19. Story
20. Street
21. Studio
22. Taxi
23. Teacher

Follow the Leader #3

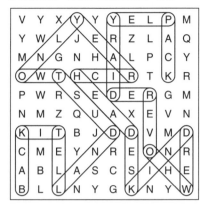

1. Back
2. Kit
3. Tell
4. Land
5. Dust
6. Two
7. Only
8. Year
9. Rich
10. Head
11. Desk
12. Kind
13. Drew
14. Who
15. Over
16. Red
17. Diary
18. Yelp
19. Pack

Hair and Bunny

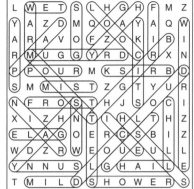

1. Bright
2. Brisk
3. Chill
4. Cloud
5. Cold
6. Cool
7. Damp
8. Drizzle
9. Dry
10. Fair
11. Fog
12. Frost
13. Gale
14. Gust
15. Hail
16. Hazy
17. Ice
18. Mild
19. Mist
20. Moist
21. Muggy
22. Pour
23. Rain
24. Shady
25. Shower
26. Sleet
27. Slush
28. Smog
29. Snow
30. Spray
31. Sticky
32. Sunny
33. Warm
34. Wet
35. Wind

Rhyme Time

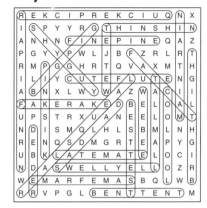

1. Bent tent
2. Best test
3. Big pig
4. Bright light
5. Cool pool
6. Cute flute
7. Fair pair
8. Fake rake
9. Fat cat
10. Fine pine
11. Fun run
12. Late mate
13. Main train
14. Pink sink
15. Quicker picker
16. Real squeal
17. Red bed
18. Sad lad
19. Same frame
20. Shy guy
21. Swell yell
22. Tall mall
23. Thin shin
24. Wee bee
25. Wet jet

House Hunting

Answer: There was no broom closet.

89

Spaced Out

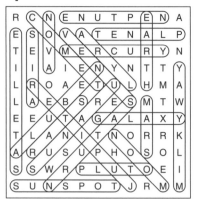

Answer:

...ran into a meteor shower.

Missing Letters #2

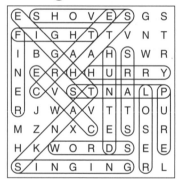

1. Pure   S
2. Singing   W
3. Hunted   A
4. Words   L
5. Shoves   L
6. Loser   O
7. Eight   W
8. Stars   T
9. Tanks   H
10. Hats   E
11. Fight   L
12. Crate   E
13. Hurry   A
14. Finer   D
15. Plants   E
16. Cave   R

Answer: Swallow the leader.

Time Out

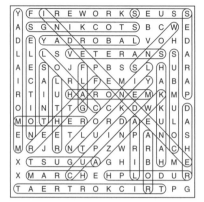

1. April
2. Arbor
3. August
4. Carol
5. Columbus
6. Cupid
7. Dasher
8. Election
9. Father
10. Fireworks
11. Flag
12. Hanukkah
13. Independence
14. Kwanza
15. Labor Day
16. Lincoln
17. Luther
18. March
19. Memorial Day
20. Menorah
21. Mother
22. Parades
23. Rudolph
24. Saint
25. Seuss
26. Snow
27. Stockings
28. Trick or treat
29. Turkey
30. Veterans

Follow the Leader #1

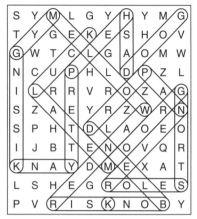

1. Good   11. Knob
2. Dash   12. Blend
3. Help   13. Drop
4. Pretty   14. Pan
5. Yank   15. Never
6. Kissing   16. Roles
7. Gym   17. Strong
8. Mellow   18. Groom
9. Wander   19. Metal
10. Risk   20. Luck

Animal Charm

Answer: It was just kidding around.

Adjective Adventure #2

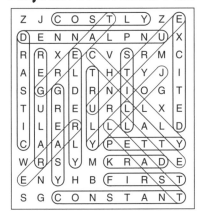

```
Z J C O S T L Y Z E
D E N N A L P N U X
R R X E C V S R M C
A E R L T H T Y J I
S G G D R N I O G T
T U R E U R L L X E
I L A E R L L A L D
C A L Y P E T T Y
W R S Y M K R A D E
E N Y H B F I R S T
S G C O N S T A N T
```

1. Chilly
2. Constant
3. Costly
4. Dark
5. Drastic
6. Elderly
7. Excited
8. First
9. Greasy
10. Great
11. Jolly
12. Late
13. Least
14. Petty
15. Rare
16. Regular
17. Still
18. Truly
19. Unplanned
20. Untrue

Unlisted "B" Words

```
B A B O O N B O A T
B A S K E T B X H S
W V B R A C E C Y A
M N L Y J B A R G E
B L I S T E R Z B B
A L Z T L E B L U A
D A Z B B T W S R N
G B A L C O N Y E A
E A R Z B A R N A N
Q Y D R A O B L U A
```

Baboon
Baby
Badge
Balcony
Ball
Banana
Barge
Barn

Basket
Bay
Bear
Beast
Beet
Belt
Berry
Bleach

Blister
Blizzard
Board
Boat
Bowl
Brace
Bureau
Bus

Missing Letters #1

```
F B E A C H C N U L
Z A M B H E A R S A
L C T X I L T I N T
W O Z H N B J J Z E
T N Y Q E W O M N M
A P M S B R I D E O
E C O P E S N S R N
R G Z W T R S A M E
T A O B X Y V M C S
V P R I C E M E S R
```

1. Same   H
2. Bacon   E
3. Serve   W
4. Lunch   A
5. Metal   N
6. Joins   T
7. Father   E
8. Power   D
9. Chin   A
10. Beach   L
11. Copes   I
12. Bride   G
13. Treat   H
14. Hears   T
15. Boat   S
16. Price   N
17. Tint   A
18. Scare   C
19. Money   K

Answer: He wanted a light snack.

Number Code

```
A B O U T A T W P
N N S L L A F E E
D H S Z H W E V T
A O H W I B O M M
N X V T E L L S O
U E H A N R B T V
G H U I L R I G I
L T M A C H I N E
Y T T E R P P Y G
```

What
movie
tells
about a
pretty
girl
who
falls
in love
with
an ugly
answering
machine?
"Beauty
and
the
Beep."

Synonym Search #2

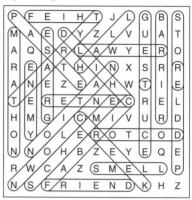

1. Barrier
2. Center
3. Child
4. Clown
5. Creek
6. Doctor
7. Enemy
8. Fabric
9. Friend
10. Grease
11. Guest
12. Hall
13. Lawyer
14. Marathon
15. Nation
16. Paste
17. Peddler
18. Scheme
19. Smell
20. Store
21. Thief
22. Truce
23. Tyrant

Do-Re-Mi

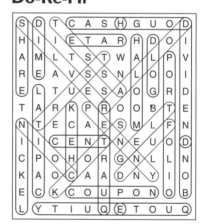

Answer: It wants to be a loan.

Slang Search

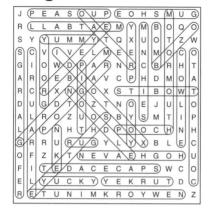

1. Bomb
2. Bozo
3. Chow line
4. Circular file
5. Couch potato
6. Glad rags
7. Gofer
8. Groovy
9. Gumshoe
10. Hog heaven
11. Idiot box
12. Main drag
13. Meatball
14. Motor mouth
15. Munchies
16. New York minute
17. Noodle
18. Nuke
19. Oater
20. Pea soup
21. Pig out
22. Pooch
23. Prexy
24. Rag top
25. Redeye
26. Rug
27. Shuteye
28. Space cadet
29. Turkey
30. Two bits
31. Yo-yo
32. Yucky
33. Yummy

Found Letters #2

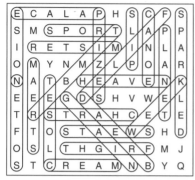

1. Failed   A
2. Prizes   Z
3. Heaven   E
4. Timber   B
5. Bread   R
6. Palace   A
7. Sweats   W
8. Noise   I
9. Mister   T
10. Charts   H
11. Fright   R
12. Canoe   O
13. Slip   L
14. Sparkled   L
15. Planet   E
16. Stream   R
17. Sport   S
18. Week   K
19. Grain   A
20. Closet   T
21. Cream   E
22. Soften   S

Answer: A zebra with roller skates

Best Quest #2

1. Beach
2. Braid
3. Clerk
4. Gasoline
5. Howl
6. Nose
7. Polar
8. Quartz
9. Queen
10. Quite
11. Recipe
12. Riot
13. Roar
14. Rough
15. Squirt
16. Sweet
17. These
18. Thief
19. Thinks
20. Unique

Play Ball

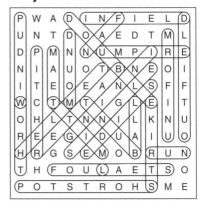

Answer: . . . wanted to go home.

Tree-mendous Fun

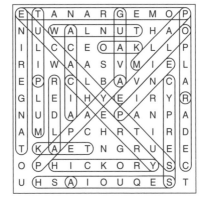

Answer: He was branching out.

Capital Fun

1. Albany
2. Atlanta
3. Austin
4. Boise
5. Boston
6. Cheyenne
7. Columbus
8. Denver
9. Dover
10. Frankfort
11. Helena
12. Honolulu
13. Juneau
14. Montpelier
15. Nashville
16. Phoenix
17. Pierre
18. Providence
19. Raleigh
20. Richmond
21. Sacramento
22. Salem
23. Santa Fe
24. Springfield
25. St. Paul
26. Topeka
27. Trenton

Follow the Leader #2

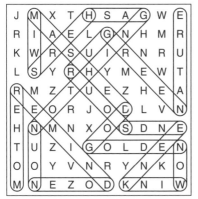

1. Mother
2. Remind
3. Dozen
4. Noun
5. Nothing
6. Gash
7. Hers
8. Swim
9. Mashed
10. Dog
11. Golden
12. Now
13. Wink
14. Knee
15. Ends
16. Sour
17. Rug
18. Green
19. Nature

School Daze

Answer: They hissed the bus.

Body Language

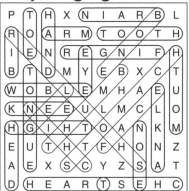

1. TH**ANK LE**ANN FOR THE PRESENT.
2. CED**AR MA**Y BE USED IN CLOSETS.
3. GRA**B ONE** BRASS RING.
4. PUT THE CO**BRA IN** ITS CAGE.
5. WHI**CH EST**ATE SHALL WE VISIT?
6. BUY LUN**CH IN** THE CAFETERIA.
7. THE ANGE**L BOWE**D TO THE CHILDREN.
8. THE **YELL**ING IS OVER.
9. TELL ME I**F ACE**S ARE HIGH.
10. WE PLAYED GOL**F IN GER**MANY.
11. WAT**CH AND** WAIT.
12. S**HE A**DDRESSED FOUR ENVELOPES.
13. T**HE ART**ICLE IS IMPORTANT.
14. WHAT DOES CHUC**K NEED**?
15. THE GINGER A**LE GOT** WARM.
16. I A**M OUT HERE**.
17. WHAT DO R**HINOS EN**JOY?
18. THIS IS THE CA**R I B**OUGHT.
19. WHERE **SHOULD ERIK** GO?
20. WAS **TOM A CHEER**LEADER?
21. WHA**T HIGH** SCHOOL DID YOU ATTEND?
22. DON'**T HUM** BEFORE BREAKFAST.
23. LET'S GO **TO** ENGLAND.
24. THEIR NAMES WERE ON THE BOS**TON GUE**ST LIST.
25. DON'T LET HIM GET **TOO THIRSTY**.

First Names (He)

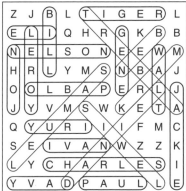

1. Albert
2. Ben
3. Bill
4. Charles
5. Daniel
6. Davy
7. Eli
8. Gene
9. Ivan
10. Jackie
11. John
12. Leroy
13. Lewis
14. Mark
15. Nelson
16. Pablo
17. Paul
18. Samuel
19. Tiger
20. Walt
21. Yuri

Code Breaker

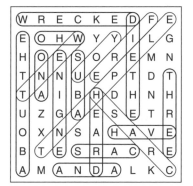

Have you heard about the elephant who went on a crash diet? He wrecked a bus, three cars, and a fire engine.

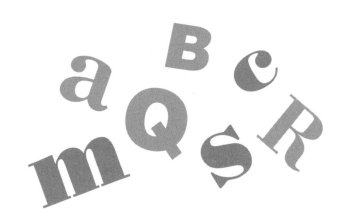

Best Quest #1

1. Bait
2. Charms
3. Cider
4. Fatter
5. Gravy
6. Guava
7. Judge
8. Juggler
9. Lazy
10. Patch
11. Pave
12. Place
13. Seat
14. Shake
15. Shivering
16. Steady
17. Stitches
18. Teacher
19. Travel
20. Truck
21. Valley
22. Verb

Music Maker

Answer: Rap Van Winkle.

Dog Daze

Answer: A beagle with lox.

Yummy!

Answer: Cheesecake.

Clothes Encounters

Answer: Wish and wear clothes.

Choices #3

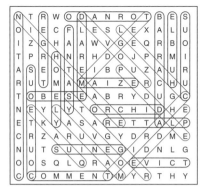

1. Barracuda
2. Chapel
3. Chariot
4. Comment
5. Concentration
6. Courteous
7. Curious
8. Devour
9. Emerald
10. Evict
11. Fantasy
12. Genius
13. Homely
14. Humble
15. Maize
16. Manual
17. Meddle
18. Midget
19. Nightmare
20. Obese
21. Orchid
22. Peddle
23. Platter
24. Quake
25. Regret
26. Stagger
27. Tornado

Index

About the Author

Helene Hovanec's parents introduced her to puzzles when she was six years old and she has been solving puzzles ever since. Ms. Hovanec is a former elementary school teacher who turned her hobby into a career. This is her 36th puzzle book. She is very involved in the puzzle world, especially with the World Puzzle Championship.

Ms. Hovanec lives in Princeton, N.J. Her two sons are grown and solve puzzles occasionally.

Other books by Helene Hovanec
available from Sterling

Around the World in 80 Puzzles
Brainteasers for Young Einsteins
Dinosaur Puzzles
Science Puzzles for Young Einsteins